MARKETING EFFECTIVENESS IN BANKING

MARKETING EFFECTIVENESS IN BANKING

Edited by
R.D. Sharma
&
Gurjeet Kaur

ANMOL PUBLICATIONS PVT. LTD.
NEW DELHI - 110 002 (INDIA)

ANMOL PUBLICATIONS PVT. LTD.
4374/4B, Ansari Road, Daryaganj
New Delhi - 110 002
Ph.: 3261597, 3278000
Visit us: www.anmolbooks.com

Marketing Effectiveness in Banking

First Edition, 2003

ISBN 81-261-1401-0

PRINTED IN INDIA

Published by J.L. Kumar for Anmol Publications Pvt. Ltd., New Delhi - 110 002 and Printed at Tarun Offset Press, Delhi.

CONTENTS

PREFACE

With the liberalization and globalisation of banking services during the last decade Bank Marketing has received considerable significance in India. Marketing of banking services implies provision of need-based schemes, at reasonable interest rates, at convenient locations and promoted through effective tools and techniques. In order to compete successfully with the challenges imposed by both domestic and foreign banks, an efficient mechanism to fulfil the banking requirements of the target clientele need to be introduced. It is through effective marketing, an individual bank can think of surviving and sustaining its business for fairly long period.

Besides, Rural Bank Marketing aims at fulfilling the banking requirements of rural populace. Rural banks have been established with the prime objective of meeting credit needs of the rural sector and as such marketing has a significant role to play in the form of collection of relevant, information from the target market, dissemination of the collected information throughout the organization and presentation of the products/services as per the requirements. Although both GOI and RBI have launched various need-based schemes at reasonable prices, but the present need of the hour is the implementation of the effective communication system due to the widespread illiteracy, ignorance, unawareness and hesitation among rural masses.

Thus, positioning of banking services entails effective communication with the optimum utilization of latest information technologies. At present banks are using new technologies to gain competitive advantage and improve profitability against their bank and non-bank competitors, viz., Telephone Banking, ATMs, PC-Home Banking etc. Henceforth marketing of banking services has become easier with the introduction and adoption of these banking technologies. In order to capture the potential of using new technologies, operations management in banking industry need to be recognized as a separate function—which transforms inputs such as personnel efforts, computers, facilities, energy and money into output viz., loans, and other supportive services.

The latest concept of bank marketing is the relationship banking, which focuses on maintaining and strengthening the banker-customer relations. In relationship marketing emphasis is on retaining the present customers than to go for attracting new ones. The logic behind this phenomenon is that the cost of attracting new customers is higher than the cost of retaining the present clientele. A bank can ensure long-term profitability if it succeeds in delivering need-based services with personal touch to its existing market.

LIST OF CONTRIBUTORS

Prof. R. D. Sharma, Head and Dean, Department of Commerce, University of Jammu, Jammu- 180006. (Jammu & Kashmir)

Dr. Umesh C. Patnaik, Professor of Commerce, Berhampur University, Berhampur–760007. (Orissa)

Dr. Debabrata Das, Lecturer, Department of Commerce, Gauhati University, Guwahati–781014. (Assam)

Dr. R. K. Gupta, Reader in Finance, DCS, Panjab University, Chandigarh–160036. (Punjab)

Ms. Shweta Gupta, Research Scholar, Department of Commerce, University of Jammu, Jammu – 180006. (Jammu & Kashmir)

Dr. Ambika Prasad Pati, Assistant Professor, Department of Commerce, Arunachal University, Itanagar–791111. (Arunachal Pradesh)

Dr. Sujit Sikidar, Professor of Commerce, Gauhati University, Guwahati–781014. (Assam)

Dr. Sandeep Tandon, Lecturer in Commerce, Directorate of Distance Education, University of Jammu, Jammu–180006. (Jammu & Kashmir)

Ms. Apara Sharma, Junior Officer, ICICI Bank, Mohali. (Punjab)

Ms. Jyoti Sharma, Research Scholar, Department of Commerce, University of Jammu, Jammu- 180006. (Jammu & Kashmir)

Sri Kalyan Mukherjee, UGC Teacher Fellow, Department of Commerce, Gauhati University, Guwahati–781014. (Assam)

Mr. Basudev Chattoi, Department of Commerce, B.A. College, Berhampur–760007. (Orissa)

Dr. Gurjeet Kaur, Lecturer in Commerce, Directorate of Distance Education, University of Jammu, Jammu—180006. (Jammu & Kashmir)

Ms. Neetu Chopra, UGC Project Fellow, Department of Commerce, University of Jammu, Jammu–180006. (Jammu & Kashmir)

Ms. Rashmi Sharma, Research Scholar, Department of Commerce, University of Jammu, Jammu–180006. (Jammu & Kashmir)

1

MARKETING ORIENTATION IN INDIAN RURAL BANKING

—R. D. SHARMA & GURJEET KAUR

Marketing Orientation [MO] is a continuous process which deals with the management's efforts to understand target customers' current and future needs and to satisfy these unfulfilled needs and expectations better and sooner than competitors [Shiffman and Kanuk 1995; Stanton, Etzel and Walker 1991; Leader and Kyritisis 1989; Enis 1980; Cundiff, Still and Govoni 1980; McCarthy 1979; Fox and Wheatley 1978; Kohli and Jaworski 1990] through inter functional coordination [Narver and Slater 1990, Kohli, Jaworski and Kumar 1992]. Thus MO can ensure long run profits, survival and success of an institution [Kotler 1996; Hartley 1983] on continual basis.

The present status of marketing orientation in Indian rural banking can be studied by evaluating the continuous efforts made by Government of India [GOI] and Reserve Bank of India [RBI] towards introducing the concept of customer orientation by creating need based time, form, place and ownership utilities [Bhattacharyay 1989] through different banking services. Both GOI and RBI have been rigorously launching several packages for the overall development of rural sector through various agencies primarily Indian Banking System to cater to the banking needs of the rural masses. In this perspective Regional Rural Banks [RRBs] were established in addition to several other rural development oriented agencies, primarily with the objective of promoting and introducing such banking services which would assist in the upliftment of socioeconomic status of rural people. The history of marketing orientation in Indian rural banking goes back to 1904 with the setting up Cooperative Credit Societies, followed by a chain of several institutions and banks viz., Cooperative Land Mortgage Bank [1929], State Bank of India, Agriculture Refinance and Development Corporation [1963] renamed in 1982 as NABARD, Agricultural Finance Corporation [1968], College of Agricultural Banking [1969], Nationalization of 14 commercial banks in 1969 and 6 in 1980, Credit Guarantee and Investment Corporation of India [1971], and Bankers Institute of Rural Development [1983].

The main objective behind the establishment of RRB's was the lack of adequate marketing culture in existing rural banking basically towards the credit needs of the small and marginal farmers, rural artisans and other weaker sections. Cooperatives failed in channelising the banking funds into productive projects and thus due to overall poor operations they faced the problems of mounting overdues. Moreover these banks covered only the credit requirements of rural populace while ignoring the deposit aspects of banking. The commercial banks suffered from limited coverage in rural sector, inadequate appraisal of rural problems and thus lacked developmental orientation. Thus on the recommendations of Banking Commission [1972] and Working Group [1975], RRBs were created to satisfy the banking requirements of rural masses.

Present level of marketing orientation in Indian rural banking has been conceptually analyzed by focusing on the basic marketing mix elements of the present relevance. In the banking industry people and procedural aspects require adequate attention [Thingalaya 1991] even though these Ps are the part of the universal four Ps of McCarthy [Kotler 1996].

PRODUCT ADEQUACY AND SUITABILITY

Here marketing orientation means that all major product decisions should begin with an understanding of the needs of the consumers [Cundiff et al. 1980; Enis 1980; Hughes 1980]. In this regard many steps have been taken by GOI and RBI to satisfy the fast changing banking product requirements of different people of rural economy.

Initially the lending services were given prime importance as compared to deposit mobilization in rural banking. From the view point of loan disbursement, the main focus had been laid on agricultural credit requirements of rural people through the setting up of Cooperative Credit Societies [1904], Cooperative Land Mortgage Bank [1920], Cooperative Central Land Mortgage Bank [1929], Agricultural Credit Department [1935]: Standing Advisory Committee on Agricultural Credit [1951], National Agricultural Fund [1956], Agricultural Refinance and Development Corporation [1968], College of Agricultural Banking [1969], whereas the needs relating to trade, commerce, industry and agricultural allied activities received secondary importance. The nationalization of major commercial banks accelerated further the pace of rural credit designed to meet the banking requirements of various sectors of rural community. Short-term agricultural needs have been successfully looked after by GOI and RBI through the establishment of cooperative banks, commercial banks, RRBs and SIDBI and long term agricultural demands by NABARD and IDBI. Furthermore Large Sized Adivasi Multipurpose Cooperative Societies [LAMPS] were organized in 1971 for providing an appropriate institutional framework in tribal areas. In pursuance of government's 15 point programme for the welfare of minority communities, a number of steps were taken by the banks for ensuring adequate credit facilities to these rural sections [RBI 1995]. The introduction of Lead Bank Scheme [1969] and Multipurpose Scheme [1972] further strengthened the concept.

The financial sector has been playing a major role in the mobilization and allocation of finance. It helps in the transfer of financial resources from the net savers to net borrowers. Thus the gains to the real sector of economy depends on how efficiently the financial sector performs this basic function of intermediation [RBI Report 1998-99]. Many institutions viz., cooperative banks, SBI, commercial banks, and RRBs have been looking after the credit needs of rural populace through the provision of call loans, term loans, cash credit, overdraft, personal loans for durable consumer goods, construction of residential houses, loans to road transport operators, loans to small scale industry, loans to self employed persons, loans to technicians, loans to retail trade, green card loan scheme [Maheshwari 1991, Mithani 1989], kisan credit card scheme and new subsidy scheme for cold storage / godown [Budget 1999]. These institutions have also been playing active role in mobilizing the savings of rural population thereby indicating the habit of saving thrift. Major portion of the bank's lending depends on the savings of the customers and thus the lending aspect of the bank primarily rests on the level of deposit mobilization. Large number of need based deposit schemes have also been introduced by RBI from time to time viz., savings deposits, fixed deposits, current deposits, cash certificates, daily saving schemes, minor saving schemes, monthly interest income scheme, annuity or retirement scheme, farmers' scheme, insurance linked deposit scheme etc. [Maheshwari 1991; Mithani 1989].

PLACE MANAGING EFFECTIVENESS

The products / services offered at the right places [Mark 1988] need to be easily accessible with infrastructural requirements as per the local competitive conditions make the physical distribution outlet of an institution marketing oriented [Ross 1997; Sharma 1995; Gupta 1992; Cundiff, Still and Govoni 1985; Fox and Wheatley 1978]. This aspect of bank marketing mix has also received due consideration of GOI and RBI through the branch expansion of the aforesaid existing agencies in the rural areas. First step in this direction has been the setting up of Cooperative Credit Societies [1904], followed by the establishment of Primary Agricultural Credit Societies and Land Development Banks. Further on the recommendation of Rural Credit Survey Committee [1954], SBI was established in 1955 to facilitate the banking services in rural areas through its extensive branch network and thereafter the nationalization of 14 major commercial banks in 1969 and 6 in 1980 provided much stimuli and sense of direction to expand their operations by opening branches in the rural areas as well. Lastly the introduction of RRBs [1975] led to a massive increase in the number of rural bank branches in the hitherto neglected areas of the rural economy. Agricultural Finance Corporation [1981] and CRAFICARD [1981] have also emphasized the branch expansion programme in the rural areas. A Committee on Financial System [19921 headed by M. Narsimham suggested that branch licensing be abolished and the matter of opening new branches be left to the commercial judgement of an individual bank. However, RBI designed to give freedom to banks to rationalise their existing extension counters. In this context, rural banks were given liberty in 1994 to relocate their loss making branches within service area only. They were also allowed to open the extension counters so as to ensure the provision of uninterrupted and satisfactory banking services on an ongoing basis to the clientele in their area of operation [1995]. Further 70 rural banks were freed in 1995 from the service area obligation and were permitted to relocate their loss making branches at taluka / block headquarters, village markets, mandis and agricultural produce centres. They were also advised to merge two loss making branches operating within the proximity of about 5 km into one branch. Subsequently they were also given operational liberty in 1997 to open and relocate branches at semi-urban and urban centers subject to the prior approval of their respective boards.

PRICE REASONABILITY

Here price mix covers both aspects of banking interest rate structure i.e. interest charged on loans and interest paid on deposits and fee, commission and other charges on different types of banking services determined within the framework of rural developmental priorities of the society. Marketing orientation demands delivery of superior products / services at the reasonable prices [Kotler 1996] and thus for ensuring overall economic development of rural sector, it is imperative that timely and adequate institutional credit at affordable cost is made available [RBI 1997]. The marketing mix in banking, being important to both bankers and their customers, has to be designed in the light of socioeconomic profile of the target market [Sharma 1995]. Evidence regarding the practice of charging high rate of interest by moneylenders in India is found in the literature of the Vedic times i.e. 2000 to 1400 B.C. and also in *Manu Samriti* which indicates that interest rates were prescribed by almost all Hindu law givers like Manu, Vasistha, Yajnavalkya and Gautama and Budhayana as also Kautilya and it used to be as high as 15% p.a. [Reddy 2000]. According to Manu and Vasistha, interest rates were neither linked to risk involved nor the purpose for which the money was borrowed but they were directly linked to the caste classification of the borrowers. Brahmin was to be charged 2%, Kshatriya 3%, Vaishya 4% and Shudra 5% per month. Chanakya's interest rate structure was risk weighted since the rate of interest increased with the risk involved in the borrowers' business. The deployment of funds by resorting to borrowing from different sources became inevitable, resulting in indebtedness on the whooping interest burden. As a result of huge indebtedness, many committees and economists concluded that the Indian farmers are born in debt, live in debt and die in debt [Reddy 200]. Even after the introduction of the Agricultural Act in 1879 and the Vsurions Loan Act in 1918, the extent of indebtedness before the Second World War amounted to Rs. 1800 crore whereas at the end of the War in 1945 it was estimated at Rs. 900 crore. Under such a situation, the only way to get rid of the maladies of indebtedness was to institutionalize credit facilities and provide liberal financial help for productive purposes at cheaper interest rates [Hooda and Turan 1993]. Thus the exorbitant rate of interest charged by unscrupulous private moneylenders was one of the major reasons behind the establishment of banks in rural sector [GOI 1945; All India Rural Credit Survey 1954; Wadhwa 1980; Kanvinde 1984; Verma 1988 and Patnaik and Mishra 1993]. Therefore government started the cooperative movement with the passing of Cooperative Credit Societies Act in 1904 [Gupta and Singh 1985; Thingalaya 1993] in order to provide banking services and facilities to rural people at the reasonable cost. Further in order to remove the non-institutional moneylenders from rural scenario, SBI, commercial banks and RRBs were introduced. Different credit agencies and debt owed by cultivator households to them reflect that the contribution of non-institutional agencies was more (1951: 92.4; 1961: 81.6; 1971: 68.3] as compared to the institutional agencies [1951: 7.6; 1961: 18.4; 1971: 31.7] [Desai 1979]. Indigenous bankers in rural areas have not paid adequate attention towards developing deposit side of their business and thus found it difficult to compete successfully with Cooperative Credit Societies in respect of attracting deposits. Nidhis and chit funds were the associations in ancient

India for mobilising rural savings [Desai 1979]. The evidence of providing interest rates on deposits and charging fee on other banking services viz., discounting of bills, issuing cheques and bank drafts, providing locker facilities etc. can be found from the advent of Cooperative Credit Societies and later on from banks established in rural India. In July 1972 the Ministry of Finance introduced a 'Differential Rate of Interest Scheme' under which the public sector banks were asked to render financial assistance to weaker sections of the community at a concessional rate of interest [4% p.a.]. Among other financial institutions set up by the GOI, RRBs have been established primarily for lending only to weaker sections and that too at a low rate of interest [Steering Committee on RRBs 1981]. Keeping in view the socioeconomic status of rural population RBI has been increasing interest rates on deposits [RBI 1991; 1992; 1995] and decreasing interest rates on advances [RBI 1992; 1993 and 1994] of commercial, cooperative and RRBs. Last in this direction has been the 'deregulation of interest rates' recommended by Narsimham Committee [1992] which provided for fixing of the minimum and maximum rate of interest by RBI. In between these limits the banks have been freed to quote the interest rates as per their banking requirements [RBI 1995; 1996; 1998].

PROMOTION OPTIMALITY

Instead of just selling [Mark 1988] what RBI directs, multifacet promotional tools in banking can educate the customers about various services designed in the light of their expectations. This aspect of marketing mix has not received much attention of policymakers and administrators of rural banks as compared to other Ps [Sharma et al. 1998]. Till date on the counter services are quite common among rural banks but field selling of banking schemes has not become very popular. Rural banking business can be promoted by making bank deposits more attractive by raising interest rates on saving account, permitting tax benefits on deposits, compensating customers for delays in collection of cheques [Committee on Customer Service 1997], interaction between the banks' staff and small scale industry borrowers [Nayak Committee 1994]. A committee on agricultural credit [1998] suggested open meetings with farmers to assess their problems and difficulties, tangible incentives to farmers who are prompt in repayment and rebate to borrowers who repay their dues promptly.

PERSONNEL DEVELOPMENT AND TRAINING

Greater marketing orientation demands greater job satisfaction and organisational commitment of employees [Stanton, Etzel and Walker 1991; Kohli and Jaworski 1990]. People mix within the conceptual framework of marketing orientation requires result oriented training to the employees to make themselves fully equipped with all the latest mechanism so as to create a congenial and healthy atmosphere in banks. RBI took initiative in 1969 by opening a College of Agricultural Bank [CAB] in Pune and later on NABARD introduced Bankers' Institute of Rural Development [BIRD], Lucknow in 1983 to meet the training needs of the cooperative banks and RRBs. Besides CAB and BIRD, many other agencies are also catering to the training requirements of rural banks' like NABARD, RRB Staff Training College, Bolpur Training Centre, Mushirabad, RRB Training Centre, Bangalore and National Institute of Rural Development [NIRD], Hyderabad. Dantwala Committee [1977], Steering Committee on RRBs [1981], Kelkar Committee [1986], Agricultural Credit Review Committee [1989] have emphasised the need of overall development of rural bank personnel through training. RBI stressed not only on the RRB offices in unbanked rural areas but also on personnel with requisite expertise and skill in these branches [RBI 1990]. Finally a Committee on Agricultural Credit [1998] headed by R.V. Gupta recommended a package of incentives to bank employees for training in prestigious institutions, educational facilities and corporate recognition of outstanding performances and also to provide weightage to these measures in promotion. It further suggested that training in institutions need to design fresh packages shifting their focus from project-based programmes to borrower appraisal including techniques for assessing the needs of the rural households.

PROCEDURAL EFFECTIVENESS

Marketing effectiveness in the form of procedural simplification and objectivity facilitates adequate and timely banking services to the clientele [RBI 1997 and 1994] so as to achieve customer satisfaction resulting into long term profits. All the rural development oriented institutions as mentioned in the product adequacy and suitability section have been set up to provide speedy and smooth flow of bank credit to rural sector. The Committee on Customer Satisfaction [1991] suggested technology upgradation and continuous review of system and procedures in light with changing needs of customers to ensure efficient and effective services viz., immediate encashment of cheques, issuance of draft, updating of saving bank passbook and issue of accounts to customers. RBI has also directed rural banks to strengthen their appraisal mechanism so that bank loans are properly and effectively disbursed [RBI 1992]. In this perspective RBI has issued various guidelines to banks with the objective of ensuring lending discipline in appraisal, sanction, monitoring and utilisation of bank finance [RBI 1998].

RELATIONSHIP MARKETING

Good relationship with customers aims at promising and delivering high quality good service and fair prices to various associated parties and is extremely effective with the right customers who get strongly committed to a specific system and expect consistent and timely service [Kotler 1996]. Impolite behaviour [Pai 1987; Vaghul 1976; Varde 1976], unfriendly and non-cooperative nature [Hebbar 1988] and negative attitude [Bhattacharya 1989] of bank staff towards customers lead to the absence of personal contacts and relationship [Mandanna and Chengappa 1993] thereby affecting the goodwill of the bank. The cooperative credit societies, SBI and commercial banks could not succeed in maintaining good customer banker relations as these institutions lacked adequate appreciation of rural problems [GOI 1975]. In this regard Narasimham Committee focussed on institution's ability in combining local feel and familiarity with the problems of rural masses and efforts for mobilising maximum deposits so that friendly atmosphere can be injected in the institution. The Committee on Customer Service (1991) suggested a well-planned approach of job enrichment to make bank personnel more responsive and customer friendly to operate successfully in a competitive environment and with team spirit [Narver and Slater 1990].

The establishment of RBI in 1935 strengthened the efforts of government in the upliftment of socioeconomic status of rural populace and from then onwards the GOI started introducing various rural development oriented schemes through RBI. Thus the aforesaid literature indicates that the GOI and RBI have taken many initiatives in introducing, modifying and withdrawing the rural banking products/services to meet the banking requirements of different rural communities. The interest rate structure and distribution outlet of rural bank branches have also been changed from time to time and designed in the light of socioeconomic profile of rural masses. Bank employees efficiency, cooperation, devotion and friendly behaviour and procedural effectiveness have also received due significance. The major aspect where less attention has been diverted is the adequate utilisation of various promotional tools. No Committee has ever been set up to cover promotional aspect of banking in India. Although GOI and RBI have taken several steps to implement the recommendations for the development of rural India through the operations of rural banks, but these initiatives are inadequate for creating and enhancing the needed marketing status and real sense of professionalism in rural banks. The establishment of an institution doesn't amount to marketing orientation unless it understands and appraises the needs of target people on continuous basis and successfully meets the same through inter-functional coordination.

REFERENCES

Bhattacharyay, Biswa N. [1989]. "Marketing Approach to Promoting Banking Services", *Vikalpa,* Vol.14 [Apr-June], No.2, pp. 35-41

Budget [1990]. Yashwant Sinha Attempts a Please, *Hindustan Times,* Sunday, 28th [February], p. 01.

Cundiff, Edward W; Richard R. Still and Norman A. P. Govoni [1980]. *Fundamentals of Modem Marketing,* New Delhi, Prentice Hall of India.

Desai, S. S. M. [1979]. *Rural Banking,* Mumbai, Himalaya Publishing, pp. 21 - 93.

Enis, Ben M [1980]. *Marketing Principles,* California, Goodyear Publishing Co.

Fox, Edward J. and Edward W. Wheatley [1978]. *Modern Marketing: Principles and Practice,* Illinois, Scott Foresman & Co. Glenview.

Goiporia, M. N [1991]. Committee on Customer Service, *RBI Bulletin,* [January], pp. 68 -69.

GOI [1945]. *Report of the Agricultural Finance Sub-Committee,* New Delhi, p. 59

Gupta, Krishan, Gopal and Rajendra Singh [1985], A New Look to Regional Rural Banks, *Khadi Gramodyog,* [December], p. 461.

Gupta, Mamta [1992]. *"Marketing Effectiveness of Banking Services: A Case Study of SBI in Jammu City",* Unpublished Dissertation, Dept. of Commerce, University of Jammu.

Gupta, R.V. [1998]. Committee on Agricultural Credit, *RBI Bulletin,* June, pp. 497—503.

Hartley, Robert F [1983]. *Marketing Fundamentals,* New York, Harper & Row Publishers.

Hebbar, C. Kusumakara [1988]. "Bank Marketing Strategy in Commercial Banks", *Southern Economist,* [October], vol. 27, pp. 17-18.

Hooda, R. P. and Turan [1993], *Rural Indebtedness - Problems, Policy Measure and Solutions,* New Delhi, Deep and Deep Publications, p. 1-2.

Hughes, G. David [1980]. *Marketing Management,* Philippines, Addison Wesley Publishing Co.

Kanvinde, D. J. [1984]. "Bank as a Lever for Rural Development", *Monthly Review,* [January], p.20.

Kohli, Ajay K. and Bernard J. Jaworski [1990]. "Market Orientation: The Construct, Research Position and Managerial Implications", *Journal of Marketing,* [April], vol. 54, pp. 1 - 3.

Kohli, Ajay K; Bernard J. Jaworski and Ajith Kumar [1992]. "A Measure of Market Orientation", *Journal of Marketing,* [December], pp. 3-4.

Kotler, Philip [1996]. *Marketing Management: Analysis, Planning, Implementation and Control,* New Delhi, Prentice Hall of India, p. 488.

Leader, W. G and N. Kyritsis [1989]. *Fundamentals of Marketing,* London, Hutchinson Education.

Madhukar, R. K. [1992]. "Dynamics of Bank Marketing", *Prajnan*, vol. XXI, no. 1, pp. 117- 18.

Maheshwari, S. N. [1991]. *Banking: Law and Practice,* New Delhi, Kalyani Publisher, pp. 259-63.

Mandanna, P. K. and P. G. Chengappa [1993]. "Marketing Approach in Rural Banking", *Economic Review,* [June], 6-8.

Mark, V. V. [1988]. "Deposit Mobilisation and Marketing of Bank Services", *Economic Review,* [June], vol. 33, no. 1.

McCarthy, E. Jerome [1979]. *Essentials of Marketing,* Illinois, Richard D. Irwin.

Mithani, D. M [1989]. *The Anatomy of Indian Banking,* New Delhi, Himalaya Publishing House, pp. 47-48.

Nayak, Committee, [1994]. "Adequacy of Institutional Credit to the Small Scale Industrial Sector", *RBI Bulletin,* [March], pp. 425-426.

Narsimham, M [1992], "Report of the Committee on Financial System", *RBI Bulletin,* [February], pp. 369 -377.

Narver, John C and Stanley F. Slater [1990]. "The Effects of a Market Orientation on Business Profitability", *Journal of Marketing,* [October], pp. 20-35.

Pai, M. R [1987]. "Customer Service in Banks", *Southern Economist,* [February], vol. 25, pp. 21-25.

Patnaik, U.C. and P. N. Mishra. [1993], *Rural Banking in India,* New Delhi, Anmol Publications, pp. 16-17.

Rangarajajan, C. [1996]. "Banking Sector Reforms", *RBI Bulletin,* [March], p. 149.

———, [1993]. "Banking Education and Training", *RBI Bulletin,* [November], p. 1365.

RBI Bulletin [1999], "Credit Control and Other Measures", January, p. 114.

———, [1998], "Credit Control and Other Measures", February, p. 201.

———, [1997] "Development of Banking Technology in India", January, p. 38.

———, [1997]. "Credit Control and Other Measures, January, p. 90.

———, [1995], "Credit Control and Other Measures", September, p. 828.

———, [1994]. "Credit Control and Other Measures", March, p.417.

———, [1993]. "Credit Control and Other Measures", November, p. 1365.

———, [1992]. "Credit Control and Other Measures", March, pp. 521 -796.

———, [1991]. "Credit Control and Other Measures", October, p. 1007.

———, [1990]. "Credit Control and Other Measures", December, p. 986.

RBI [1954], *Report of the All India Rural Credit Survey,* vol. II, pp. 167-174.

Reddy, Y. V. [2000]. "Future of Rural Banking", *RBI Bulletin,* [January], p. 47-48.

Sharma, R. D. [1995]. "Marketing Effectiveness in American Banks", *Prajnan,* vol. XXIV, p. 153.

Sharma, R. D. Desh Bandhu and Gurjeet Kaur [1998]. "Marketing Orientation Strategy for Rural Banks - A Case Study", *Prajnan,* National Institute of Bank Management, Pune, vol. XXVII, no. 1 [Apr-June], pp. 47-58.

Stanton, J. William, Michael J. Etzel and Bruce J. Walker [1991], *Fundamentals of Marketing,* New Delhi, McGraw Hill, p. 8.

Thingalaya, N. K. [1991]. "The Dynamics of Bank Marketing", *Economic Review,* [June], pp. 5-6.

Thingalaya, N. K. [1993]. "Role Responsibilities of Financial Institutions", *Economic Review,* [August - October], vol. 38, no. 1, p. 01.

Vaghul, N [1976]. "Employees Development for Efficient Customers Service", *Prajnan,* [April - June], vol. VI, pp. 172-75.

Varde, S. D [1976]. "Customer Service for Banks", *Prajnan,* [January - March], vol. V, no. 1, pp. 134-37.

Verma, M. L [1998], *Rural Banking in India,* Jaipur, Rawat Publication, p. 6.

Wadhwa, Charan D. [1980]. *Rural Banks and Rural Development,* Madras, Macmillan, pp. 1-3.

2

A CONCEPTUAL FRAMEWORK OF RELATIONSHIP MARKETING IN BANKING INDUSTRY

—R. D. SHARMA & GURJEET KAUR

INTRODUCTION

The basic emphasis of the McCarthy's four P's is on designing, delivering and marketing products that will win new customers and such an enterprise is known as "offensive marketing". While winning new customers is vital to the long-term success of any organisation, many firms have come to realise that survival and profits also are critically dependent upon retention of customers i.e., "defensive marketing". During the last decade, firms recognised the importance of not only attracting new customers but also of retaining them as long-term partners. The great population and economic growth of the post-World War II era, when marketing concepts were first redefined, have led to much slower growth. However, customer demands for improved quality and rapid technological developments have resulted into shortened product life cycles and intense global competition. Companies can no longer afford to replace those who have become dissatisfied and left. As a result, customer retention and development of long-term relationships have become the focus of many companies (Rust, Zahorik and Keiningham

1999), which is basically termed as Relationship Marketing (RM).

Relationship marketing is the process of developing co-operative and collaborative relationship with customers. Customer retention, being the core element of relationship marketing, includes activities such as after marketing and post-treatment satisfaction services, frequent user benefits, customer-focused care programmes, database maintenance, support for on-going relationship with customers, and programmes to involve customers into the design, development and sales activities (Naidu, Parvatiyar, Sheth and Westgate 1999). Essentially the relationship marketing provides individualised service, although the products themselves are not typically individualised.

In relevance to banking, relationship marketing entails two-way relationship between two individuals, viz., the banker and customer within the framework of a business contract. Such a business contract relating to banking operations and services begins the moment a customer opens an account with a banker. Bankers are like physicians, businessmen, lawyers, teachers and others who deal in personal, but economic services (George 1989).

NATURE AND SCOPE

Relationship marketing demands longer and deeper commitment on the part of the sellers to the buyers' success, which also includes promises, made to customers beyond the terms of payments. It creates reasons for the customers to recognise the seller more than a source for meeting many needs. Relationship marketing is not just the repetition of transactions; rather it is the interdependence and interactions to provide joint outcomes, subsequent mutual reactions and future outcomes that make a relationship (Anderson and Weit 1989; Ganesan 1994). Panigrahy (2000) focused on the importance of database and the capability to organise, analyse and segment it to make a relationship work. It requires complete and potential customers and ability to tailor marketing programmes to individual customers based on customers' characteristics and preferences thereby customising the products.

Relationship marketing strategy overcomes service intangibility (Berry 1983) and may be suitable for services that are difficult for customers to evaluate even after purchase and use (Zeithaml 1981). With predominant relationship marketing strategy, price competition is reduced.

Alexander (1979) while focusing on the nature of RM, defines relationship banking as "the internal management of all the bank's resources so that the customers' needs are identified and served by the entire institution as though it was a single, unified coordinated entity. The internal organisation and its complexities should be invisible to the customer—how it does so, should be irrelevant to him".

Banker-customer relationship entails value addition and the areas where the customers expect value efficiency from banks are cash transactions, passbook updating, speedy service like clearing, good behaviour, pleasant interior of branch office, efficient service, honesty and transparency in dealings and competitive price (Kannan 1996).

OBJECTIVES

Relationship marketing aims at building long-term relations with customers, suppliers, and distributors in order to retain their long-term preferences and business. Marketing accomplishes this by delivering high-quality products and services at reasonable prices to other parties. It builds strong economic, technical and social bonds among the parties. The final outcome of relationship marketing is the building of a unique and strong marketing network, which consists of the company and its supporting agencies with whom it has constructed / intends to construct profitable business relationship (Kotler 2000).

In a fast changing dynamic world, customers feel themselves more confused, frustrated and dissatisfied not with the existing products/services but with the decision making process because they do not have the time and expertise to make best decisions. In order to avoid such a situation or to overcome with such problems, a special kind of relationship can be maintained, which one is having with lawyers, accountants and other professionals. Within the domain of advisory relationship, a consumer expects the advisor to make decisions on his behalf; because he feels himself comparatively less effective in doing so and trusts that advisor will act in his best interests (Bos and Stodin 1994).

The final outcome of relationship marketing is customer retention. Higher retention means higher market share, which in turn means higher revenues. Moreover, sales calls are more productive with familiar customers than with new ones. In particular, a retention orientation requires firms to be responsive to customer concerns by keeping open dialogues with them. This approach involves effective programmes for receiving and responding to complaints; active solicitation and analysis of customer satisfaction data, and the development of long-term strategic relationships with customers by meeting their changing needs.

For establishing an efficient network of relationship banking many initial and final requirements have to be fulfilled. The initial requirements are viz., (i) management commitment; (ii) relationship identification; (iii) establishing responsibility for overall co-ordination; (iv) evolving and development of appropriate co-ordination methods; (v) motivation among bank employees.

Thus a relationship banking strategy always aims at capturing the customer relationship, so that the customer concentrates all products and services with a single seller (Bos and Stodin 1994).

IMPORTANCE

Relationship marketing has received increasing interest over the past years. In the marketing literature, concepts such as inter-firm relationships, buyer-seller relationships and alliances have been significantly used to describe different alternatives to the traditional transactional selling (Hangland 1999).

Traditionally the company's focus was on attracting new customers and terminating the relation with the completion of sales task, but now greater emphasis has been shifted towards the retention of customers because "one estimate is that attracting a new customer can cost five times as much as pleasing an existing one and it might cost sixteen times as much to bring the new customer to the same level of profitability as the lost customer. Customer retention is thus more important than customer attraction". (Kotler 2000, p. 22). Berry (1983) also asserted that the cost of attracting or acquiring new customers may exceed investments made in retaining the current ones. The key to customer retention is customer satisfaction as such a highly satisfied customer stays loyal longer; buys more as the company introduces new products and upgrades existing products; talks favourably about the company and its products; pays less attention to competing brands and less sensitive to price; offers product or service ideas to the company; and costs less to serve than new customers. This task of creating strong customer loyalty results into relationship marketing. Gronroos (1990) related the satisfaction of a customer (determined by service quality) with the strength of the relationship with the company, and this leads to longevity of relationship and relationship opportunities. Socio-emotional (intimacy) benefits also facilitate strength to the relationship and imply sharing of vital information, sharing socially and psychologically (Fehr and Russell 1991).

The importance of relationship banking lies in securing high-value relationships in which customers consolidate total bank product usage in one bank, thereby implying all of a customer's business now and in the future with a particular bank. High value relationship banking enables banks to facilitate proactive service process to selected customers, converting them into highly profitable clients and retaining their business for years to come. As such high-value relationship tends to be very profitable; the introduction of a business process that consolidates all of a customer's business with one financial institution can enhance shareholder value.

TECHNIQUES AND ELEMENTS

Relationships are maintained by techniques such as direct mail, telephone calls, personal visits. It basically depends on four dimensions products/services that will build loyalty; employees who are adept at relationships; appropriate set of customers; and measures to monitor and improve (Panigrahy 2000).

The success of relationship banking rests on certain factors viz., trust, commitment, complaint handling, customer satisfaction, customer loyalty, salesperson, periodic needs reassessment, staying in touch, purchase reinforcement and personal touches. **Trust** is an important factor in the development of marketing relationships and prevails where a customer has confidence in a seller's reliability and integrity (Morgan and Haunt 1994). Holmes and Rampel (1987, p.199) observe, "Trust is strengthened if partners are responsive in ways that acknowledge an individual's particular needs and affirm their sense of worth". Trust in a person is acquired by assessing the previous interactions, such as conflicts; the partner has had with others in similar situations (Holmes 1991).

Satisfaction with complaint handling is related positively to trust (Stephen, Brown and Chandrashekaran 1988). **Commitment** also focuses on long lasting desire of parties to maintain a relationship (Morgan and Haunt 1994). Kelly, Donnelly and Skinner (1990, p.322) states that "the organisational commitment of service customers is indicative of the organisation's likelihood of developing or maintaining customer identification with organisational goals and values and retaining the service customer as an active participant in the service encounter". The concept of commitment becomes relevant to services due to the need for customer participation in the delivery process. Like trust satisfactory complaint handling is also related positively to customer commitment. **Effective complaint handling** results in efficient management of customer relationships in service businesses. Complaint handling helps in maintaining and developing these relationships because of challenges in managing quality, important role played by customer loyalty drives profitability (Berry and Parasuraman 1991). The attitudinal and behavioural consequences of **customer satisfaction** play an important role in developing long-term customer relationships. Highly satisfied customers remain loyal for longer period, which ultimately give strength to the relationship between the concerned parties. Customer's preference for a particular brand or a company for quite significant period reflects his loyalty towards that brand / company, which in turn signifies positive attitude for building and retaining the relationship. **Service salesperson** is the primary contact for the customers both before and after the purchase due to the uncertainty resulting from the salesperson's ability to reduce perceived uncertainyy (Zeithaml 1981). Thus relationship quality consists of at least two dimensions, (i) trust in the salesperson (e.g., Swan, Trawick and Silva 1985) and (ii) satisfaction with the salesperson (e.g., Crosby and Stephens 1984). The strong ties of relationship between partners largely depend on the frequency with which the salesperson communicates with customers and the quality enhances with salesperson competency. Product knowledge and market awareness often lead to customer satisfaction, with sales people with higher expertise and referent power are viewed more trustworthy among customers. Efforts to **"stay in touch"** with the customers have been determined as a key factor of relationship maintenance in service sector, viz., insurance (Crosby 1984), wholesale banking (Greenwich Associates 1987) and many other. Parties cannot be expected to trust each other, if a particular moment constitutes their only opportunity to interact. In order to build strong relationship, customers expect **periodic assessment** of their needs and assurance that they have made correct purchases. Finally, **personal touch** such as cards, gifts etc., can go a long way in establishing and maintaining concrete relationship among respective parties. Relational sellers are prone to express their cooperative intentions to the customers. Long-term service exchange sometimes demands for mutual resolution of tedious problems.

The activities of the banking industry are all about "relationship" where the two parties to the relationship are the bankers and the customers. It is an interactive, face to face relationship between a bank and an individual on one to one bases. Information technology is playing its role in the banking industry, but it is only an aid to the employees across the counter, ultimately the success depends on the better and efficient services extended to the customers. A bank customer expects good service with smile, service with efficiency, service with speed and service with value addition. In order to provide good services, bank staff must possess certain qualities, which include knowledge of bank, fair perception about the future, clarity of objectives, awareness of their contribution to the attainment of corporate goals, a very high acumen about profit issues and above all, exceptional capacity towards handling inter-personal relationships (Kannan 1996).

The banking sector needs to become more customers focused instead of product-centric. Staff has to understand the needs of customers as individuals, so that such information can be used to improve the quality of service they offer. There has to be greater emphasis on training to ensure staff uses the technology in ways appropriate to particular types of relationship (Calder 2001).

STRATEGIC ACTION

Kumar (1999) suggested following marketing strategies for introducing and maintaining relationship banking:

1. Customer relation programmes aimed at providing an opportunity to the customers to meet Branch Manager, controlling authority / senior functionaries of the bank to highlight their grievances and give suggestions for further improvement of service should be initiated.
2. Customers are more sophisticated than they were 10 or 20 years ago. To capture more business, we must equip ourselves well with the knowledge required for our job, so that we can convince customers about the comparative advantage of our schemes when compared with those of our competitors.
3. The minor matters like non-supply of chequebooks/ account opening forms etc., on time, can cause lot of inconvenience / irritation to the customers. Thus, ensuring prompt supply of customer-oriented stationery can help in retaining the customers for fairly long time.
4. Relationship marketing either through personal contact or direct mail, is an important element in

the marketing mix of any bank. There should be a continuous effort in all banks to enhance skills that will build relationship across all customer segments.

5. The internal organisation can be a source of strengths. The culture in some banks—its shared values (i.e., service to the customer is first priority) and its norms of behaviour (i.e., respond promptly to any customer complaint) can be so strong and positive that it provides the basis for a sustainable competitive advantage; conversely, it can be a source of weakness. Bank's top management should lay out a series of business directions that will enhance bank's strengths and differentiate it from competitors.
6. Total quality management (TQM) is the path towards the goal of customer satisfaction. This, however, calls for change within people. Banks, who pay a lot of attention to customer satisfaction, will emerge from any adversity in better shape. TQM requires mapping the series of tasks that take place in the business development. They also need to eliminate those steps that are ineffective, inefficient or inflexible from the customer's perspective if properly applied and used, TQM would allow banks to reduce their costs and create a legion of loyal customers.
7. Quality circles may be introduced at branches where customers' service needs urgent improvement so as to associate the dealing staff. Formation of quality circles should be marketed to the staff. They provide a unique opportunity to satisfy the self-esteem requirements of the employees at the grass-root and motivate them to participate in improving the total performance of any organisation and the quality of

their own work-life. In the present context of the imperative necessity for every bank to enhance productivity and improve quality of services and enable them to face the many challenges to come, for their survival, this new and innovative concept of "quality circle" will require active participation of the employees in the area of problem recognition and analysis, together with implementation of corrective measures.

8. Complaint cell should be activated at head office / zonal office and customers' grievances should be redressed expeditiously. To minimise recurrence of such complaints, analysis of complaints should be conducted periodically region-wise and activity-wise and remedial measures should be taken by branches/ controlling authorities / senior functionaries at head office.
9. Restructuring of branch networks more towards customer orientation is also necessary. This restructuring of branch networks, as the point of contact between individual customer and bank has become a considerable challenge to banks due to the need for more intense relations with customers.
10. Customers meet, exclusively for corporate customers, at important business centres should be arranged and their problems / difficulties should be solved expeditiously.

REFERENCES

Alexander, Errol D. (1979) "Focus on Relationship Banking", *Bankers Magazine,* 162(2).

Anderson, Erin and Barton A. Weitz (1989),"Determinants of Continuity in Conventional Industrial Channel Dyads," *Marketing Science, 8* (Fall), pp.310-323.

Berry, Leonard L. (1983), Relationship Marketing, in L.L.Berry, G.L.Shostack, and G.D.,Upah, (eds.) *Emerging Perspectives on Services Marketing,* Chicago: American Marketing Association, pp.25-28.

Bos, David and Hicholas Stodin (1994),"A New Benchmark in Relationship Banking," *The Bankers Magazine,* Vol.177 (September-October), No.5, pp.45-48.

Calder, David (2001),"Now It's Even More *PERSONAL" Scottish Banker,* (April), pp.26-29.

Crosby, Lawrence A. (1984), *Consumer Attitudes Toward Whole Life Insurance,* Atlanta: Life Office Management Association, p. 52.

Crosby, Lawrence A. and Nancy Stephens (1987), "Effects of Relationship Marketing on Satisfaction, Retention and Prices in the Life Insurance Industry," *Journal of Marketing Research,* Vol.XXIV (November), pp. 404-411.

Ganesan, Shankar (1994),"Determinants of Long-Term Orientation in Buyer-Seller Relationships," *Journal of Marketing,* 59 (April), pp. 1-19.

George, C.T. (1989), "Controversial Banks and Customer Service", *Times of India,* 26 (October), p.6.

Gronroos, Christian (1990), *Service Management and Marketing: Managing the Moments of Truth in Service Competition,* Lexington MA: Lexington Books, p. 138.

Kotler, Philip (2000), *Marketing Management: Analysis, Planning, Implementation and Control,* New Delhi, The Prentice Hall of India Ltd.

Kumar, L.N. (1999), *Strategic Marketing of Banking Services,* New Delhi, Suneja Publishers.

Morgan, Robert M. and Shelby Hunt (1999) "Relationship - Based Competitive Advantage: The Role of Relationship Marketing in Marketing Strategy," *Journal of Business Research, 46* (April), pp.281-290.

Naidu, G. M. Atul Parvatiyar; Jagdish N. Sheth and Lori Westgate (1999),"Does Relationship Marketing Pay? An Empirical Investigation of Relationship Marketing Practices in Hospitals," *Journal* of *Business Research* 46 (April), pp. 207-218.

Panigrahy, Dibakar (2000),"Relationship Marketing: An Opportunity for Bankers in the Next Millennium," in Raghavachari, M. and K.V. Ramani (ed.), *Delivering Service Quality—Managerial Challenges for the 21st Century,* New Delhi, Macmillan India Ltd, pp. 85-91.

Stephen S. Tax; Stephen W. Brown and Murali Chandrashekaran (1998), "Customer Evaluations of Service Complaint Experiences: Implications for Relationship Marketing", *Journal of Marketing*, Vol. 62 (April), pp.60-76.

Zeithami, Valarie A. (1981), "How Consumer Evaluation Processes Differ Between Goods and Services", in J.H. Donnelly and W.R. George (eds.), *Marketing of Services,* Chicago: American Marketing Association, pp. 186-190.

3

MARKETING EFFECTIVENESS IN INDIAN CONSUMER BANKING

—R.D. SHARMA & MS. NEETU CHOPRA

Effectiveness in any managerial function is a performance appraisal measured in terms of level and quality of success from the concerned working record and / or survey of evaluative opinion of the success of the organisation in question during a specific period i.e. it evaluates the nature and quality of relevant work carried on within predefined parameters set for achieving the goals. Marketing effectiveness (ME] refers to the quality of managerial efforts in improving and maintaining product/service performance for achieving customer satisfaction and institutional goals within the given situation (Sharma 1995], as it is not always only sales or profit performance (Kotler 1994] which measures the marketing effectiveness of a business enterprise. The marketing efforts continue for competitive advantage along with improvement, change, diversification, modification and expansion etc., of the business and as such the effectiveness of these efforts always remain under the supervision and control of marketing management as it is a never ending process due to its nature of slow learning and fast forgetting (Kotler and Levy 1971]. The efforts are planned, designed and carried on within the framework of relationship between product performance and customer expectations in terms of product suitability, price reasonability, place managing effectiveness and marketing communication so as to provide right product, at the right time and at right place to the customers with effective prior communication to them which are broadly known as marketing mix (McCarthy 1971]. Customer expectations originate from exposure, experience and marketing communication and thus, they act as standards against which the customers evaluate the product / service performance and they derive high expectation due to the changing needs and wants, the company's promise and delivery of superior performance and competitors' promise to do still better. Therefore, it is necessary for the companies to correctly understand the customer expectations and provide improved performance to match those expectations, which ultimately result in customer satisfaction and expand the marketing operations (Godeswar 2000]. Such an exercise needs constant vigilance to keep the customer satisfied, loyal and motivated towards product / service along with the speed and nature of change in customer expectations and level of competition.

It is in this context that marketing effectiveness in Indian consumer banking has to be achieved through such efforts which read the target market, distinguish the business opportunities, choose the best market segments, continue to offer them superior services and finally maintains that each marketing mix variable plays a vital role in the overall efficiency of a bank (Sharma 1995]. Therefore, before summarising the concept of marketing effectiveness in Indian consumer banking the nature of exchange process in consumer banking, profile of the parties involved, and the marketing efforts need to be studied in detail.

EXCHANGE PROCESS IN CONSUMER BANKING

Exchange process in consumer banking exists between the consumer banks and the banking customers for the exchange of needed banking services in lieu of the price the customer pays to the banks in different forms. Thus, the exchange process has three basic components viz., consumer banks, bank customers and the consumer banking services which are common to the interest of both the parties i.e. bankers and their customers. Consumer banks are those banking institutions which provide banking services like deposit schemes, loan facilities, bank drafts and collection of cheques etc. to the ultimate customers i.e., such people who need the aforesaid banking services for ultimate consumption and not for business purposes. All these three components of exchange process are discussed as under.

INDIAN CONSUMER BANKS

In India all the commercial banks, rural banks, cooperative banks, post office and even some of the non-banking financial institutions are extending consumer-banking services. But for the present study the banking services extended by commercial and rural banks are evaluated in terms of their quality of marketing efforts. The ongoing process of liberalisation and globalisation of banking services has placed consumer banks in a new phase of competition causing a series of changes in the industry due to vibrant market situation. Such an emerging new dynamic environment necessitates planned marketing efforts of total business concept of marketing to meet fast increasing demand of effective consumer banking services otherwise they will continue to face a number of threats like struggle for existence and extinction etc. (Beim 1992 and Garwood 1992]. In view of intense competition in the banking industry all over the world, Indian consumer banks are applying marketing techniques in their operations. The marketing techniques in banking are increasingly gaining significance in developing countries like India due to greater demand for cost reduction and quality services. Indian consumer banking primarily regulated and controlled under the provisions of the Banking Regulation Act, 1949 and Reserve Bank of India Act, 1934 is under the governance and supervision of both central and state governments. The commercial banking of both private and public sectors is under the supervision of central government while regional rural banks are under the joint supervision of both centre and state governments.

The commercial banking system in India consists of both scheduled and non-scheduled banks. Scheduled banks are those banking institutions whose banking affairs are not conducted in a manner detrimental to the interest of its depositors and aggregate value of paid up capital and reserves not less than 5 lakh and non-scheduled banks are those institutions which are not included in the second schedule of RBI. As on July 12, 2000, 297 scheduled commercial banks were operating in the country whose aggregate deposits and loans outstanding were estimated as Rs. 8.5 lakh crore and Rs. 4.6 lakh crore respectively, with the credit deposit ratio of 54.6%. Along with the aforesaid commercial banks 196 Regional Rural Banks (RRBs] are also operating in 427 districts with 14497 branches in the country (Sharma et al.1998] channalised a total credit of nearly Rs. 10,000 crore. The priority sector bank credit has increased from 13% of net bank credit in 1969 to more than 42% in 1995.

INDIAN CUSTOMERS OF CONSUMER BANKING SERVICES

Customers of Indian consumer banking services i.e. ultimate bank customers, who buy banking services for household and / or individual purposes and not for any business or non-business organisation, of different socioeconomic backgrounds need variety of banking services for their day to day banking requirements. India having more than 100 billion of population with male: female ratio of 52 : 48, with literacy rate of 52.11 % (1991 Census], about

74% of whom living in more than 6 lakh villages, 40% still below poverty line, with female and male literacy percentage of 39.42 and 63.86 respectively and having about Rs. 13192.6 per capita income (net national income] at current prices in 1997-98, has tremendous scope for consumer banking services. The various consumer-banking services are saving and loan schemes and other supportive services.

Today customers of banking services in India from both rural and urban areas are quite demanding. Though majority of rural customers are illiterate but the savings from rural areas are more as compared to that of urban areas. They need multifaceted banking services like multipurpose deposit schemes, finance for various corps, purchase of tractors, minor irrigation, purchase of land for agricultural purposes, loan for household requirements, allied activities like diary etc. Today customers from urban areas need the banking which are fully aimed at the promotion of consumerism, upgrading of technology in terms of services, easier handling of routine jobs, simple loan instalments, credit card facilities etc. (Sundaresan 1994]. Owing to the increased competition among banks of demanding customers, they find themselves with the task of differentiating their products/services as a method of attracting new customers.

Moreover customers expect banks equipped with global expertise, superior service, fully computerised operation, electronic payment system, ATM, and ability to respond to market changes. Thus the marketing efforts of consumer bankers are always subject to change due to changing customer needs. Customer satisfaction is the prime and most important objective of every bank in the competitive environment (Sharma]. To compete with it banks concentrate on such services to the target customers, which give them maximum satisfaction, enhance the goodwill of the bank and keep it fit at the market place.

MARKETING EFFORTS OF INDIAN CONSUMER BANKS

The marketing efforts in consumer banking services are planned, designed, improved and monitored with regard to all marketing mix variables consistently as per on going consumer banking requirements of the market within the framework of socioeconomic priorities of the government vis-a-vis legal provisions. The overall marketing efforts work as an index of marketing effectiveness and operational efficiency in each of marketing mix elements of Indian consumer banking.

PRODUCT ADEQUACY AND SUITABILITY

Product mix in consumer banking refers to all those banking products, which are developed and monitored consistently in the light of fast changing requirement of bank customers. Such products may be developed, designed and monitored centrally within the regulation but their delivery differs from situation to situation and from bank to bank. Thus the quality in delivery of banking products/services is determined on the spot when customer himself is face to face with bankers. The process of building banking product mix in India though started about one hundred years before when indigenous banks were extending credit services to the people but the real breakthrough came up with the enactment of Banking Regulation Act, 1949. The RBI in consultation with state and central governments formulate the banking policy with regard to all issues including product mix adequacy and suitability. It is never ending process of determining and interpreting consumer needs and then modifying standards, procedures and policies to meet these needs both qualitatively and quantitatively (Sharma 1995]. With the changing marketing situation of liberalised market oriented economy, making transactions more transparent and establishing an effective regulatory framework. As a result consumer banks in

India are providing timely and adequate number of needed services to the customers and due to technological advancement, mass communication, rapid transportation, banks are reaching the customers at door steps with a good package of product / services because the customers, due to vast spread of education, fast electronic services, growing consciousness, modern banking customers are becoming more informed about latest product development and are becoming more choosy (Jha 2001]. There is quite tough competition among the consumer banks including foreign, domestic, private and public sector banks and other financial institutions for achieving more market share and profitability and accordingly to achieve the market economy in such a competitive environment. Bankers are innovating good range of products / services like call loans, term loans, cash credit, overdraft, kisan credit scheme, saving deposit schemes, retirement schemes (Maheshwary 1991, Mithani 1989], automated teller machines, consumer credit cards, farm credit cards, traveller's cheque, merchant banking, mutual funds, housing finance etc. By providing these services the customer banking target of the Indian consumer banking system is becoming very strong. Customers need more than one account and that too in more than one bank e.g. besides saving bank account, modern bank customers need fixed or recurring deposit account also (Thingalaya 1996]. To remain competitive, banks have to adopt a technology driven culture, better control and monitoring system, build skill to innovate and market new products. By adopting product-oriented strategy, they can innovate their service techniques with the speed of response, which is today the new competitive weapon for achieving market economy.

PRICE REASONABILITY IN CONSUMER BANKING

A right product at right place cannot sell well till it is

suitably priced. Price refers to the amount of money a customer is willing to pay for the services but in broader sense it includes more than money (Stanton et. al. 1994]. Due to multiplicity of banking services price takes many forms like interest on loans, annual charges for credit cards or certain deposit schemes, service charges for closing an account before a prescribed period, ATM charges, monthly fee, minimum balance, balance inquiry fee and fee for deposit and / or loan statements. Low interest on deposit is not the apparent price as it is not the price paid by the customer but the bank pays it to him. In fact in this case customer forgoes the immediate liquidity by depositing the money in the bank and even he loses the opportunity of putting it in more attractive schemes.

Pricing in banking sector is most powerful marketing tool but pricing strategy has limited scope in banking sector because of control exercised by the RBI. In banking, price is always designed in the light of socioeconomic profile of target market (Sharma 1995]. Different firms charge different prices for identical products in different channels such as retailing, mail order or the Internet etc. In India, banks also price their products / services differently depending upon the convenience of the customers to pay for these services. Today Indian banking customers are becoming more organised, aggressive and awakened. Their demographic and environmental factors like income, family composition, the location of competing branches also have an impact upon the customers' willingness to pay for these services, upon the bank's pricing strength and its ability to attract customers. Today banks are pricing their services differently depending on whether the customer uses them through the Internet or a branch office (Zettelmeyar 2000]. Since banking services cannot be resold, the decision made by banks regarding their price will not impose restriction on their difference.

After the introduction of financial sector reforms in 1991,

the market situation of Indian consumer banking became more vibrant and as a result banks are facing a series of changes. One of the immediate changes that the banks are confronted with is the deregulated interest rate regime from the administered interest rate era (Sunderasan 1994]. At present there are only two rates of interest prescribed - one for lending purpose and second for deposits. After deregulation rates of interest on loans to the priority sector have been reduced. Interest rates for loans over Rs. 2 lakh have been regulated, while the small loans up to Rs. 2 lakh in priority sector continue to be governed by regulated rates of interest. Financial sector reforms in banking sector results in various changes like convertibility of rupee on current account, rationalisation of tax structure, reduction of duties, discouraging direct credit, reducing Cash Reserve Ratio (CRR] and Statutory Liquidity Ratio (SLR] and introduction of prudential and capital adequacy norms etc. After these changes, customers of Indian consumer banking services today are compelled to keep high balances, budget for increased account cost or to give up bank's account altogether.

PLACE MIX DECISIONS

Marketing orientation facilitates availability of the right products at the right places easily accessible to the target markets (Sharma 1996, Madhukar 1992]. With the opening up of Indian economy, some of the Indian consumer banks feel uncomfortable due to traditionally managed mix decisions because today automation is of significant importance to the present consumer banking customers. Indian banks are facing challenges due to fast computerisation, mechanisation, modernisation of their work culture, drive-in-counters, telebanking, anywhere banking, electronic fund transfer and clearing system etc. These are some of the latest developments, which are catching the sight of the customers, and they are dealing with banks from home, office or even from the car

(Shanbhag 1997]. These changes have reduced the annual requirements of bank branches for traditional bank manpower, space and layout arrangement etc. And its rise is primarily due to successful implementation of computer-based system for all types of banking operations. The factors like residential development; transportation and traffic patterns etc., enable the banks to ascertain the number of potential customers, type of products demanded and likely gross margins. Reduction or increase in the size of these variables will automatically increase or decrease in the geographical area necessary to support a particular bank branch. Customers generally choose branches in an endeavour to have sufficient convenience with regard to branch working hours, extent of traffic congestion near branch, distance from home or work place and it's functioning. Indian banks today are connecting their branches in a specified area to service centres to attend the customer banking needs regarding deposits, loans and other routine services. These service centres with the upgradation of technology are connected to the main branch through computer network and they are servicing the target segments more efficiently and proving to be cost and time effective (Sundaresan 1994].

With the recent reforms in financial sector as per ongoing liberalisation and globalisation (Thingalaya 1995], the commercial banks in India are growing in size to meet the fast changing socioeconomic goals of Indian economy. They grown into unwieldy size with spread of branches from just 8,262 in 1969 to 62,270 in 1996 geographically far and wide by bringing down the per branch population of 64,000 to about 11,000 during this period. These branches are expanding working hours, extending routine services round the clock, instead of waiting for the customers to visit the bank, the banks visit the customer's home for business and remain always keen to know more and more about customers so that needed changes are expected in the service package (Mishra 2001]. Besides geographical coverage, the customer banks design better internal organisational structure both in rural and urban areas along with needed modification in the channels for the distribution of their products / services making better relations with their customers, establishing smaller outlets at village markets / mandis and agricultural produce centres at different villages to fulfil the agricultural needs of the village people (RBI 1996]. The Narasimham Committee (1992] suggested the replacement of branch licensing system with the commercial judgement of an individual bank for setting up a new branch. Besides RBI extended freedom to banks to rationalise their existing branch network by relocating branches, setting up of controlling offices and establishing extension counters. It is because of the economic independence of large geographical area, the policy of providing autonomous status to the public sector banks. In addition to 25 old private sector banks, 9 more private sector banks have been established (RBI 1999]. Changes in the banking policy further facilitated the creation of a competitive environment. To compete effectively with the private sector and non-banking companies, the Indian commercial banks are undertaking newer activities like investment banking, securities trading, insurance business, technology driven culture, facilitating the implementation of MIS and due to the importance of transportation and communication, more mobile population, the Indian consumer banks are establishing more and more branches in different parts of the country to bring down per office population significantly.

MARKETING COMMUNICATION EFFECTIVENESS

New Millennium provides both opportunities and challenges for the financial sector in general and banking sector in particular and as a result banks have to depend upon effective marketing communication through advertising, personal selling, sales promotion and regular interactions with customers (RBI 1999]. Today the Indian banking customers come across many advertisements in print media because the use of radio, television and outdoor advertisement fail to make out a clear advertising message. Beside the banks and various other financial companies are using net advertisements for marketing banking products through banners on web sites (Kamalaveni 1999]. In the present age of brand proliferation and highly competitive market scenario, Indian banks are using various promotional techniques such as they are conducting customer relations programmes, setting up customer service departments at the head office, organising customer service campaigns and door to door surveys to attract the potential customers and today they are using cyber space to bring users and the products together. They are also offering branch system in different areas and adding innovative value to their products. They are raising interest rates on saving bank deposits. Permitting tax benefits (Committee on Customer Service 1999]. Internet banking is also becoming a key to promote the banking operations through direct contact with potential buyers and to build a relationship with them for future action (Sheshunoff 2000]. With the use of computer system and networking satellite communication through Videsh Sanchar Nigam Ltd. (VSNL: The Internet Service provider in India] in banking operations (Mirash 1999], the banks can conduct meetings with customers; arrange exhibitions, personal contact to motivate them to use these services. Banks today are adopting information technology based market approaches (RBI 2000] to maintain interactive communication with their customers and to make them aware about the products offered by the banks, sharing market information about the competitors' products in the market (Tripathi 2000]. In order to make unique image of the banks in the minds of the customers, Indian banks involve themselves in publicity like press releases or public activities on the one side and on the other they are giving training to bank staff to tackle the computer-based operations and to handle the potential customers.

TRAINING AND DEVELOPMENT OF BANK PERSONNEL

The managerial competence and quality of human resources in Indian consumer banks can only be achieved by regular review of their recruitment policies, by proper motivation for work and by proper training and development of the personnel (RBI 1997] in the light of growth of information technology and computerisation of banking operations. The introduction of computerised clearing of cheques, international communication system of SWIFT and with the growing volume of banking transactions necessitates to lay emphasis on improved customer service and better management control (RBI 1993]. Various disintermediation pressures arising from liberalised capital market have also changed the overall banking operations such as they have shifted from traditional banking services to various other new services on Net, lowest cost for customers, faster turnaround and customized Internet help desk etc. Keeping in view the fast changing technological environment, today banks are increasingly turning to the use of computer based programs, they are focussing on careful selection of manpower required, proper manpower planning and proper implementation of their plans (Kothai 1995]. They are offering computer assisted learning courses, appropriate training packages, more cost effective ways of imparting training to new recruits by using technologies such as computer, audio, video and special courses before their induction (RBI 1993] to make them effective, responsive, motivated and friendly to operate in a competitive environment (Rangarajan 1993]. The increased network system has also enabled the customers to know more about the quality of life across and they have to increasingly take more responsibilities (Nagabrahmam 1995]. Just Citibank's 33% of its 1,90,000 customers who migrated to Internet banking in India in a short span of six months indicates that today both banking customers and bankers are aware about the technological changes and there is a need to lay emphasis on high quality personnel in banking industry (RBI 1997]. A committee was also set up in the year 1994 by RBI to establish an institute on banking technology with the objective of imparting high level technology training to bankers and for offering professional level courses (1994]. An early step was taken in 1969 in this direction to focus on the training needs of middle and senior level personnel in banking industry by establishing an institute viz., National Institute of Bank Management (1996]. To meet the training and development needs of bank personnel, SBI has also brought in needed changes in its recruitment, induction, training, performance appraisal and stressing more on innovative schemes, restructuring continuous monitoring of activities etc. (Nagabrahmam 1995]. The State Bank Institute of Information and Communication Management set up in 1990 could train about 12,500 bank personnel by 1997 in the light of changing technological environment. Besides these institutes, many other agencies like RBI Staff Training College, Chennai, Bankers' Training College Mumbai, and Bankers' Institute of Rural Development Lucknow, College of Agricultural Banking are also catering to the training requirements of various banks (RBI 1993] for the creation and monitoring of good work culture to achieve institutional goals along with competitively best services to the customers (RBI 1996]. Training institutions of the banks need to divert their attention from project based training programs to those, which includes training for assessing the needs of various customers in different areas.

REFERENCES

Beim, David (1992). "Why Are Banks Dying," *Colombia Journal of World Business* (spring), p.1.

Chadha, B.L. (1995). "Emerging Scenario of Rural Banking in India," *Quarterly Economic Journal of Syndicate Bank,* vol. 40. 2, (November - January), pp. 2 -12.

Darshan, Murali E. (1999)."Information Technology - The Moderen Tool for Effective Marketing," *Indian Journal of Marketing,* vol. XXIX no. 4 - 6 (April - June).

Garwood, Griffith, L (1992), "CRA Regulations Gain New Respectability", *The Bankers Magazine* (May -June), p. 39.

Godeswar, B. M. (2000). "Gaining Marketing Advantages Through Superior Customer Value," in M. Raghavchari and K.V. Ramani, (eds.), *Delivering Service Quality: Marketing Challenges for 21st Century,* New Delhi, Macmillan, pp. 42 - 49.

Goiporia, M. N. (1991). "Committee on Customer Service," *RBI Bulletin,* January, pp. 68 -69.

Kamalaveni, D. (199). "Internet—An Emerging Medium of Advertising," Indian *Journal of Marketing,* vol. XXIX, no. 4-6 (April - June), pp. 10 -11.

Kothai, Krishna (1995). "HRD: Rural Banking," *Pigmy Economic Review,* vol. 40, no. 4 (May-July), pp. 11 -12.

Kotler, Philip (1994). *Marketing Management,* New Delhi, Prentice Hall, p. 756.

——— (1977). "From Sales Obsession to Marketing Effectiveness," *Harvard Business Review,* (November - December), p. 69.

———, and Sindndy J. Levy (1971), "Demarketing, Yes Demarketing," *Harvard Business Review,* (November - December), p. 75.

Madhukar, R.K. (1992). "Dynamics of Bank Marketing," *Prajnan,* vol. xxi, pp. 117-118.

McCarthy, Edman Jerome (1971). *Basic Marketing: A Managerial Approach,* Homewood.

Mirash, O.S. (1999). "Role of Computers in Local Administration," *Kurukshetra - The Monthly Journal on Rural Development*, vol. 47, no. 7 (April), pp. 13-14.

Mishra, A.K. (2001), "Banking Sector Reforms in India" in Subhash Garg (ed.), *Emerging Issues in Financial Sector,* Jaipur, Arishant, pp. 153 -160.

Nagabrahmam, D. (1995). "Human Resource Development for Banking Sector," *Pigmy Economic Review)* vol. 40, no. 4 (May - July), pp. 1 - 7.

Narsimhan, M. (1992). "Report of the Committee on Financial System", *RBI Bulletin* (February), pp. 369 - 377.

RBI (2000). "Economic Growth, Banking and Information", *RBI Bulletin,* vol. XIV, no. 9 (September), pp. 933 - 938.

———, (1999). "Banking Development and Policy Perspectives", *Report on Trend and Progress of Banking in India,* December, pp. 1-39.

———, (1999). "Development in Commercial Banking", *Report and Progress of Banking in India,* (December), pp. 59 - 63.

———, *Universal Banking: Supervisory and Regulatory Aspects,* p. 147.

———, (1997). *Development of Banking Technology,* vol. II, no. 1 (January), pp. 38 - 43.

———, (1996). *Composition and Ownership Pattern of Bank Deposit,* vol. II, no. 12, pp. 961 - 963.

———, "Banking Sector Reforms", *RBI Bulletin,* (March), pp. 148 -156.

Shanbhag, N. A. (1997). "Second Banking Revolution Competing for the Future", *Pigmy Economic Review Journal of Syndicate Bank,* vol. 42, no. 4, (January), p. 5 - 7.

Sharma, R. D. (1995) . "Marketing Effectiveness in American Banks," *Prajnan,* vol. XXIV p. 153.

———, (1991). Marketing of Banking Services of Transnational Banks in India, *The IDEA International,* vol. 1 (July - December), pp. 15 -19.

———, Desh Bandhu, and Gurjeet Kaur (1998), "Marketing Strategy for Rural Banking: A Case Study," *Prajnan,* vol. XXVII, no. 1, (April - June), pp. 47 - 58.

Sheshunoff, Alex (2000). "Winning CRM Strategies," Chayanika - A *Transcription service from SBI Staff College,* Hyderabad, vol. Ill, no. 2.

Sundaresan, R. (1994). "Indian Banking in Retrospect and Prospective View," *Pigmy Economic Review,* (May - July), vol. 38, no. 4, pp. 4-8.

Thingalaya N. K.(1996). "Proliferation of Banking in India— Some Less Known Facts," *Pigmy Economic Review,* (May - July), vol. 41, no. 4, pp. 6-7.

———, (1995). "Success Stories of Social Transformation Through Banking Played Down," *Quarterly Economic Journal of Syndicate Bank,* vol. 40, no. 3, (February- April), pp. 1-2.

Tripathi, B. D. (2000). "Agricultural Extension Personnel in New Millennium—A Prospective View," *Yojana*, vol. 44, no. 7 (July), pp. 46-48.

Stanton, William J, Machael J. Etzel and Bruce J. Walker (1994). *Fundamentals of Marketing,* New Delhi, McGraw Hill, p. 296.

4

SELLING OF BANKING PRODUCTS: ISSUES BEFORE ONLINE BANKING

—SUJIT SIKIDAR & KALYAN MUKHERJEE

INTRODUCTION

The Banking Service and its products have been sold to the customers in a diversified manner under the context of satisfaction in Banking Services and technological improvement brought about. In addition to the banking products and services have been put to severe test owing to the emergence of Internet in Banking Services. Considering the above facts, it will be very pertinent to conduct an analysis into the challenges posed by online banking upon its products and services which the said article attempts to ponder over.

ESSENTIALS OF ON-LINE BANKING SERVICES

Banks have traditionally been in the forefront of harnessing technology to improve their products, services and efficiency. They have, over a long time, been using electronic and telecommunication networks for delivering a wide range of value added products and services. With the introduction of Personal Computer (PC), easy access to Internet and World Wide Web(WWW), Internet is increasingly used by banks as a channel for receiving instructions and delivering their products and services to their customers. This form of banking is generally referred to an Internet Banking.

On-line banking services has three essential elements, those are:

(*i*) The Basic Level Service which is the bank's websites which disseminate information on different products and services offered to customers and members of a public in general. It may receive and reply to customers' queries through e-mail.

(*ii*) Simple Transactional Websites which allow customers to submit their instructions, applications for different services, queries on their account balances, etc., but not permit any fund-based transactions on their accounts. And

(*iii*) Fully Transactional Websites which allow the customers to operate on their accounts for transfer of funds, payment of different bills, subscribing to other products of the bank and to transact purchase and sale of securities, etc.

Apart from the aforesaid elements of on line banking, some other distinctive features are:

(*i*) It resumes the traditional geographical barriers as it could reach out to customers of different countries/ legal jurisdiction.

(*ii*) It has added a new dimention to different kinds of risks traditionally associated with banking, heightening some of them and throwing new risk control challenges.

(*iii*) Security of banking transactions, validity of electronic contract, customer's privacy, etc. which have all along been concerns of both bankers and supervisors have assumed different dimentions given that Internet is a public domain, not subject to control by any single authority or group of users.

(*iv*) It poses a strategic risk or loss of business to those banks who do not respond in time, to this new technology, being the efficient and cost effective delivery mechanism of banking services.

(*v*) A new form of competition has emerged both from the existing players and new players of the market who are not strictly barks.

THE GROWTH OF ONLINE BANKING

Online banking or Internet Banking is a product of e-commerce in the field of banking and financial services. In what can be described as Business to Consumers or B 2 C domain for banking industry. Internet Banking offers several online services like balance enquiry, requests for cheque books, recording stop-payment instructions, balance transfer instructions, account opening and other forms of traditional banking services. Banks are also offering payment services on behalf of their customers who shop in different shops, e-mail etc. The new concept of banking is still evolving and banks are repositioning themselves based on new emerging online banking model. Online banking through Internet has presented regulators and supervisors worldwide with new challenges. The Internet, by its nature, reaches across borders and is, for this reason, engaging the attention or regulatory and supervisory authorities all over the world.

Online banking through the Internet, both as a medium of delivery of banking services and as a strategic tool for business development, has gained wide acceptance internationally and is fast catching up in India with more banking revolution with net banking having already been unvailed. At present, the total Internet users in the country are estimated at 9 lakhs. However, this is expected to grow exponentially to 90 lakhs by 2003. Only about 1 per cent of Internet users did banking online in 1998. This increased to 16.7 per cent in March 2000. The growth potential is therefore, immense. Further incentives provided by banks would dissuade customers from visiting physical branches, and thus get 'hooked' to the convenience of arm-chair banking. The facility of accessing their accounts from anywhere in the world by using a home computer with Internet connection is particularly fascinating to Non-Resident Indians and High Networth Individuals having multiple bank accounts.

EMERGENCE OF BANKING PRODUCTS AND SERVICES IN 21ST CENTURY

Banks in India are at different stages of the web-enabled banking cycle. Initially, a bank, which is not having a web site, allows its customer to communicate with it through an e-mail address; communication is limited to a small number of branches and offices which have access to this e-mail account. With the gradual adoption of Information Technology, the bank puts up a web-site that provides general information on the banks, its location, services available e.g. loan and deposits, application forms for downloading and e-mail option for enquiries and feedback. It is largely a marketing or advertising tool. For example, Vijaya Bank provides information on its web-site about its NRI and other services. Customers are required to fill in applications on the Net and can later receive loans or other products requested for at their local branch. A few banks provide the customer to enquire into his demat account (securities/shares) holding details, transaction details and status of instructions giving by him. These web sites still do not allow online transaction for their customers.

Some of the banks permit customers to interact with them. Such services include request for opening of accounts, requisition, for cheque books, stop payment of cheques, viewing and printing statements of accounts, movement of funds between accounts within the same bank, querying on status of requests, instructions for opening of Letters of Credit and Bank Guarantees etc. These services are being initiated by banks like ICICI Ltd., HDFC Bank Ltd., Citibank, Global Trust Bank Ltd., UTI Bank Ltd., Bank of Madura Ltd., Federal Bank Ltd. etc. Recent entrants in Internet banking are Allahabad Bank (for its corporate customers through its 'Allnet' service) and Bank of Punjab Ltd., State Bank of India has announced that it will be providing such services soon. Certain banks like ICICI Bank Ltd., have gone a step further within the transactional stage of Internet banking by allowing transfer of funds by an account holder to any other account holder of the bank.

Some of the more aggressive players in this area as ICICI Bank Ltd., HDFC Bank Ltd., UTI Banks Ltd. and Bank of Punjab Ltd. offer the facility of receipt, review and payment of bills on-line. These banks have tied up with a number of utility companies. The 'Infinity' service of ICICI Bank Ltd. also allows online real time shopping mall payments to be made by customers. HDFC Bank Ltd. has made e-shopping online and real time with the launch of its payment getway. It has tied up with a number of portals to offer business-to-consumers (B2C) e-commerce transactions. The first online real time e-commerce credit card transaction in the country was carried out on the Easy3shoppe.com shopping mall, enabled by HDFC Bank Ltd. on a VISA Card. Banks like ICICI Bank Ltd., HDFC Bank Ltd. etc are thus looking to position themselves as one stop financial shops. These banks have tied up with computer training companies, computer manufacturers, Internet Service Providers and portals for expanding their Net banking services and widening their customer base. ICICI Bank has set up a web based joint venture for on-line distribution of its retail banking products and services on the Internet, in collaboration with Satyam Infoway, a private ISP through a portal named as icicisify.com. The customer base of www.satyamon line.com portal is also available to the bank. Setting up of Internet kiosks and permeation through the cable television route to widen customer base are other priority areas in the agendas of the more aggressive players. Centurion Bank Ltd. has taken up equity stake in the teauction.com portal, which aims to bring together buyers, sellers, registered brokers, suppliers and associations in the tea market and substitute their physical presence at the auctions announced.

Banks providing Internet banking services have been entering into agreements with their customers setting out the terms and conditions of the services. The terms and conditions include information on the access through user-id and secret password, minimum balance and charges, authority to the bank for carrying out transactions performed through the services, liability of the user and the bank, disclosure of personal information for statistical analysis, non-transferability of **the fotally, motion and determination** etc. The race for market supremacy is compelling banks in India to adopt the latest technology on the Internet in a bid to capture new markets and customers. HDFC Banks Ltd. with its 'Freedom-the e-age Saving Account' Service, Citibank with 'Suvidha' and ICICI Bank Ltd. with its 'Mobile Commerce' service have tied up with cellphone operators to offer Mobile Banking to their customers. Global Trust Bank Ltd. has also announced that it has tied up with cellular operators to launch mobile banking services. Under Mobile Banking services, customers can scan their accounts to seek balance and payments status or instruct banks to issue cheques, pay bills or deliver statements of accounts. It is estimated that by 2003, cellular phones will have become the premier Internet access device, outselling personal computers. Mobile banking will further minimise the need to visit a bank branch.

Further, with the process of dematerialisation of shares having gained considerable ground in recent years, banks have assumed the role of depository participants. In addition to customers' deposit accounts, they also maintain demat accounts of their clients. Online trading in equities is permitted by SEBI. This is still another area which banks are keen to get into. HDFC Bank Ltd., has tied up with about 25 equity brokerages for enabling third party transfer of funds and securities through its business-to-business (B2B) portal, 'e-Net'. Demat account holders with the bank can receive securities directly from the brokers' accounts. The bank has extended its web interface to the software vendors of National Stock Exchange through a tie-up with NSE. IT - the infotech arm of the exchange. The bank functions as the payment bank for enabling funds transfer from its customers' account to brokers' accounts. The bank is also setting up net broking arm, HDFC Securities, for enabling trading in stocks through the web. The focus on capital market operations through the web is based on the bank's strategy on tapping customers interested in trading in equities through the Internet. Internet banking or online banking is thus promises to become a popular delivery channel not only for retail banking products but also for online securities trading.

COMPUTER NETWORKING FOR OFFERING BANKING PRODUCTS

The purpose of computer networking is sharing of computing resources and data across the whole organisation and the outside world. Computer Networks can be primarily divided into two categories based on speed of data transfers and geographical reach. A local area network (LAN) connects many services and workstations within a small geographical area, such as a floor or a building. Some of the common LAN technologies are 10 MB Ethernet, 100 MB Ethernet, 1 GB Ethernet, Fiber Distributed Data Interface (FDDI) and Ahynchronous Transfer Mode (ATM). The data transfer rates here are very high. They commonly use broadcast mode of data transfer. The Wide Area Notwork(WAN), on the other hand, is designed to carry data over great distance and are generally point to point. Connectivity in WAN setup is provided by using dial-up modems on the Public Switched Telephone Notwork (PSTN) or leased lines, VSAT networks, as Integrated Services Digital Network (ISDN) or T1 lines, Frame Relay/ X.25(Permanent Virtual Circuits), Synchronous Optical Network (SONET), or by using Virtual Private Networks(VPN) which are software-defined dedicated and customized services and used to carry traffic over the Internet. The different topologies, technologies and data communication protocols have different implications on safety and security of services.

Products

The data transmission protocol suit used for the Internet is known as the Transmission Control Protocol/ Internet Protocol (TCP/IP). The Internet is primarily a network of networks. The networks in a particular geographical area are connected into a large regional network. The regional networks are connected via a high speed "back' bone". The data sent from one region to another is first transmitted to a Network Access Point (NAP) and are then routed over the backbone. Each computer connected to the Internet is given a unique IP address (such as 142.16.111.84) and a hierarchical domain name (such as cse.iitb. ernet.in). The Internet can be accessed using various application level protocols such as FTP(File Transfer Protocol), Telnet (Remote Terminal Control Protocol (HTTP). The protocols run on top of TCP/IP. The most innovative part of the Internet is the World Wide Web (WWW). The web uses hyperlinks, which allow users to move from any place on the web to any other place. The Web consists of web pages, which are multimedia pages composed of text, graphics, sound and video. The web pages are made using Hypertext Markup Language (HTML). The web works on a client-server model in which the client software, known as the browser, runs on the local machine and the server software, called the web server, runs on a possibly remote machine. Some of the popular browsers are Microsoft Internet Explorer and Netscape Navigator.

Banking Products

Internet banking applications run on diverse platforms, operating systems and use different architectures. The product may support centralized (bank-wide) operations or branch level automation. It may have a distributed, client server or three tier architecture based on a file system or a DBMS package. Moreover, the product may run on computer systems of various types ranging from PCs, open (Unix based) systems, to propriotary main frames. These products allow different levels of access to the customers and different range of facilities. The products accessible through Internet can be classified into three types based on the levels of access granted:

Information only Systems

General-purpose information like interest rates, branch locations, product, features, FAQs loan and deposit calculators are provided on the bank's web (WWW) site. The sites also allow downloading of application forms. Interactivity is limited to a simple form of 'e-mail'. No identification or authentication of customers is done and there is no interaction between the bank's production system (where current data of accounts are kept and transactions are processed) and the customer.

Electronic Information Transfer System

These systems provide customer-specific information in the form of account balances, transaction details, statement of account etc. The information is still largely 'read only'. Identification and authentication of customer takes place using relatively sample techniques (like passwords). Information is fetched from the Bank's production system in either the batch mode or offline. Thus, the bank's main application system is not directly accessed.

Fully Transactional System

These systems provide bi-directional transaction capabilities. The bank allows customers to submit transactions on its systems and these directly update customers accounts. Therefore, security and control system need to be strongest here.

REGULATORY FRAMEWORK TO BE COMPLIED WITH IN AN ONLINE BANKING

Security

Security in Internet banking comprises both the computer and communication security. The aim of computer security is to preserve computing resources against abuse and unauthorised use, and to protect data from accidental and deliberate damage, disclosure and modification. The communication security aims to protect data during the transmission in computer network and distributed system.

Authentication

It is a process of verifying claimed identity of an individual user, machine, software component or any other entity. For example, an IP Address identifies a computer system on the Internet, much like a phone number identifies a telephone. It may be to ensure that unauthorised users do not enter, or for verifying the sources from where the data are received. It is important because it ensures authorization and accountability. Authorization means control over the activity of user, whereas accountability allows us to trace uniquely the action to a specific user. Authentication can be based on password or network address or on cryptographic techniques.

Access Control

It is a mechanism to control the access to the system and its facilities by a giving user up to the extent necessary to perform his job function. It provides for the protection of the system resources against unauthorized access. An access control mechanism uses the authenticated identities of principle and the information about these principles to determine and enforce access rights. It goes hand in hand with authentication. In establishing a link between a bank's internal network and the Internet, we may create a number of additional access points into the internal operational system. In this situation, unauthorized access causes destruction, alterations, theft of data or funds, compromising data confidentiality, denial of service etc. Access control may be of discretionary and mandatory types.

Data Confidentiality

The concept of providing for protection of data from unauthorized disclosure is called data confidentiality. Due to the open nature of Internet, unless otherwise protected, all data transfer can be monitored or read by others. Although it is difficult to monitor a transmission at random, because of numerous paths available, special programs such as "Sniffers", set up at an opportune location like Web server, can collect vital information. This may include credit card number, deposits, loans or passwork etc. confidentiality extends beyond data transfer and include any connected data storage system including network storage systems. Password and other access control methods help in ensuring data confidentiality.

Data Integrity

It ensures that information cannot be modified in unexpected way. Loss of data integrity could result from human error, intentional tempering, or even catastrophic events. Failure to protect the correctness of data may render data useless, or worse, dangerous. Efforts must be made to ensure the accuracy and soundness of data at all times. Access control, encryption and digital signatures are methods to ensure data integrity.

Non-Repudiation

Non-Repudiation involves creating proof of the origin or delivery of data to protect the sender against false denial by the sender that the data has been sent. To ensure that a transaction is enforceable, steps must be taken to prohibit parties from disputing the validity of, or refusing to acknowledge, legitimate communication or transaction.

Security of Audit Trial

A security audit refers to an independent review and examination of system's records and activities, in order to test for adequacy of system controls. It ensures compliance with established policy and operational procedures, to detect breaches in security and to recommend any indicated changes in the control, policy and procedures. Audit Trial refers to data generated by the system, which facilitates a security audit at a future date.

LEGAL PROVISIONS TOWARDS ONLINE BANKING

The legal framework for banking in India is provided by a set of enactments, viz. the Banking Regulations Act, 1949, the Reserve Bank of India Act, 1934, and the Foreign Exchange Management Act, 1999. Broadly no entity can function as a bank in India without obtaining a license from Reserve Bank of India under Banking Regulations Act, 1949. Different types of activities which a bank may undertake and other prudential requirements are provided under this Act. Accepting of deposit from public by a non-bank attracts regulatory provisions under Reserve Bank of India Act, 1934. Under the Foreign Exchange Management Act, 1999, no Indian resident can lend, open a foreign currency account or borrow from a non-resident, including non-resident banks, except under certain circumstances provided in law. Besides these, banking activity is also influenced by various enactments governing trade and commerce, such as, Indian Contract Act, 1872, The Negotiable Instruments Act, 1881, Indian Evidence Act, 1872, etc.

Online banking through Internet is an extention of the traditional banking, which uses Internet both as a medium for receiving instructions from the customers and also delivering banking services. Hence, conceptually, various provisions of law, which are applicable to traditional banking activities, are also applicable to Internet banking. However, use of electronic medium in general and Internet in particular in banking transactions, has put to question the legality of certain types of transactions in the context of existing statute. The validity of an electronic message/document, authentication, validity of contract entered into electronically, non-repudiation etc., are important legal questions having a bearing on electronic commerce and Internet banking. It has also raised the issue of ability of banks to comply with legal requirements/ practices like secrecy of customers account, privacy, consumer protection etc., given the vulnerability of data/information passing through Internet. There is also the question of adequacy of law to deal with situations which are technology driven like denial of services/data corruption because of technological failure, infrastructure failure, hacking, etc. Cross-border transactions carried through Internet pose the issue of jurisdiction and conflict of laws of different nations.

The dichotomy between integration to trade and finance over the globe through e-commerce and divergence of national laws is perceived as a major obstacle for e-commerce/i-banking and has set in motion the process of harmonization and standardization of laws relating to money, banking and financial services. A major initiative in this direction is the United

Nations Commission on International Trade Law (UNICITRAL)'s Model law, which was adopted by the General Assembly of United Nations and has been recommended to the member nations for consideration while revising/adopting their laws of electronic trade. So far India is concerned, Govt. of India has enacted The Information Technology Act, 2000, in order to provide legal recognition for transactions carried out by means of electronic data interchange and other means of electronic communication, commonly referred to as 'electronic commerce'. The Act, which has also drawn upon the Model Law, came into force with effect from October 17, 2000. The Act has also amended certain provisions of the Indian Penal Code, the Indian Evidence Act, 1872, The Bankers Book of Evidence Act, 1891 and Reserve Bank of India Act, 1934 in order to facilitate e-commerce in India.

In the course of providing online banking through the Internet, the banks in India are facing new challenges relating to online opening of accounts, authentication, secrecy of customers accounts, non-repudiation, liability standards and consumer protection etc., each of which has been examined in the context of existing legal framework.

Online Opening of Account

The banks providing Internet banking service, at present are only willing to accept the request for opening of accounts. The accounts are opened only after proper physical introduction and verification. This is primarily for the purpose of proper identification of the customer and also to avoid benami accounts as also money laundering activities that might be undertaken by the customer. Supervisors work over, expect the Internet banks also to follow the practice of 'know your customer'.

As per Section 131 of the Negotiable Instruments Act, 1881 (the Act) a banker who has in good faith and without negligence received payment for a customer of a cheque crossed generally or specially to himself shall not, in case the title to the cheque proves defective, incur any liability to the true owner of the cheque by reason only of having received such payment. The banker's action in good faith and without negligence have been discussed in various case laws and one of the relevant passages from the judgement of Justice Chagla in the case of *Bapulal Premchand Vs. Nath Bank Ltd.* (AIR 1946 Bom. 482) is as follows:

> "Primarily, inquiry as to negligence must be directed to find out whether there is negligence in collecting the cheque and not in opening the account, but if there is any antecedent or present circumstances which aroused the suspicion of the banker then it would be his duty before he collects the cheque to make the necessary enquiry and undoubtedly one of the antecedent circumstances would be the opening of the account. In certain cases failure to make enquiries as to the integrity of the proposed customer would constitute negligence".

The introduction of a new customer by a third party reference is a well recognised practice followed by the banks before opening new accounts in order to prove the reasonable care and absence of any negligence in permitting the new customer to open the account. Further, in order to establish the reasonable care the banks have to make enquiries about the integrity/reputation of the prospective customer. It is not mere enquiry about the identity of the person. The Group, therefore, endorses the practice presently followed by the banks in seeking proper introduction before allowing the operations of the customers' accounts. In the context of online banking through the Internet, and after the coming into force of the Information Technology Act, 2000, it may be possible for the banks to rely on the electronic signatures of the introducer.

But this may have to await till the certification machinery as specified in the Information Technology Act, 2000 comes into operation.

Authentication

One of the major challenges faced by banks involved in Internet banking is the issue relating to authentication and the concerns arising in solving problems unique to electronic authentication such as issue of data integrity, non-repudiation, evidentially standards, privacy, confidentiality issues and the consumer protection. The present legal regime does not set out the parameters as to the extent to which a person can be bound in respect of an electronic instruction purported to have been issued by him. Generally, authentication is achieved by what is known as security procedure. Methods and devices like personal identification numbers(PIN), code numbers, telephone PIN numbers, relationship numbers, passwords, account numbers and encryption are evolved to establish authenticity of an instruction. From a legal perspective, the security procedure requires to be recognised by law as a substitute for signature.

The banks may be allowed to apply for a license to issue digital signature certificate under Section 21 of the Information Technology Act, 2000 and become a certifying authority for facilitating online banking through the Internet.

Mode of payment under the Income Tax Act, 1961: Section 40A(3) of the Income Tax Act, 1961, dealing with the deductible expenses, provides that in case where the amount exceeds Rs. 20,000/-, the benefit of the said section will be available only if the payment is made by a crossed cheque or a crossed bank draft. One of the services provided by the banks offering Internet banking services is the online transfer of funds between accounts where cheques are not used, in which the above benefit will not be available to the customers.

Secrecy of Customer's Account

The existing regime imposes a legal obligation on the bankers to maintain secrecy and confidentiality about the customer's account. The law at present requires the banker to take scrupulous care not to disclose the state of his customer's account except on reasonable and proper occasions. Internet banking services at present are being provided by most of the banks by systems which are only accessible through "secure zone" or SSL(Secure Stockets Layer) to secure and authenticate the user through a secure browser. Most of the banks have adopted 128 Bit strong encryption which is widely accepted worldwide as a standard for securing financial transaction.

Apart from the above mentioned legal provisions, RBI has also furnished some new guidelines for online banking through the Internet, the highlight of the same is mentioned as follows:

(*i*) The Technology and Security Standard will include: Designation of network and database administration.

(*ii*) Security policies should be duly approved by the Board of Directors. Security officers exclusively for IT division which will be audited by Information system auditors.

(*iii*) To introduce logical access control techniques with user ID, passwords, smart cards or biometric techniques, and also a proxy server firwell.

(*iv*) To introduce Public Key Infrastructure(PKI)—most favoured technology. Banks may also employ outside experts or "Ethetical Hackers" for the same.

(*v*) There should be proper system of storage of backup data.

(*vi*) To ensure banks against unauthorised transfer of customers account through hacking and denial of services due to technological failure as the

Customer Protection Act, 1986 defines the rights of customers.

(*vii*) Only the banks with licenses supervised in India and with a physical presence in India shall be allowed to perform online banking through the Internet with residence of India.

(*viii*) Banks must seek prior permission from the RBI, before offering online banking through the Internet.

(*ix*) RBI guidelines on "Risk and Controls in Computers and Telecommunications" will also be applicable to online banking or I. Banking.

(*x*) Only institutions who are members of cheque clearing systems in the country will be permitted to participate in inter-bank payment get-ways for Internet payments.

(*xi*) Banks should disclose risks, responsibilities and liabilities of customers through disclosure template.

(*xii*) Hyperlinks from bank's websites should be allowed only to those portals with which they have payment arrangements.

REFERENCES

1. Information from the Internet: RBI web site: www.rbi.org.in
2. *Economic Times*, Kolkata Edition, vide dt. 8th of July, 2001.

5

MARKETING OF BANKING SERVICES IN THE NEW REGIME—SEARCH FOR A STRATEGY

—SUJIT SIKIDAR & DEBABRATA DAS

Services' marketing is one of the latest dimensions of the broad concept of marketing emerging during recent time. It was only 1980s, when the services marketing attracted attention of the corporate world owing to the rapid growth in the services sector. Marketing of financial services has become most significant constituent of services marketing in the recent past due to opening up of the economies integrating the national financial market with the global financial market. Now-a-days sophisticated marketing approach has become indispensable for every player of financial market to survive in the competitive global market. "To make capital work harder and earn more" is the slogan of today's financial markets and greater knowledge of investment products and services and better information is the common need for both investors and the institutions seeking to serve them. In order to win investors' confidence, institutions dealing with financial products must consciously endeavour to highlight the terms and conditions crucial to investment decision i.e. rate of return, repayment schedule, liquidity and benefits etc. This is where the importance of marketing emerges.

MARKETING OF BANKING SERVICES

Marketing of banking services and products is still a new area of attention. Banks put a very little attention in marketing their services up to 1960s. Although with the increase of competition in the early part of 1970s, considerable efforts were made on sales promotion and advertising, but these efforts were confined to sales only and not on the marketing. Effectiveness of selling which comes from customer satisfaction was not much emphasized during that time. Much emphasis was given on making transaction or "catching customer". A survey conducted in 1970 by the American Bankers Association concluded that a formal marketing department existed only among 55 per cent of the banks of USA. During 1970s, and thereafter there was an upsurge in the uses of marketing tools for selling banking services and instruments in the USA, UK, Canada, Germany etc. Systematic marketing efforts were initiated by the banks only in the 1980s with better understanding about market segmentation, product development and most importantly customer satisfaction. In mid 1980, banks started launching some customer care programme namely "putting the customer first", "smile campaigns" aimed at making the customers loyal to them.

INDIAN SCENARIO

In India the early initiative regarding marketing of banking services came from the State Bank of India which re-organized itself in 1972 on the basis of major market segments. Under this system, the potential and existing customers were classified in the basis of their major economic activity and they carved out and identified major market segment viz., commercial and institutional, small industries and small business, agricultural and farm activities and personal and services. With the arrival of the 1990s accompanied by liberalization of economy, financial sector reforms, sudden explosion of mutual funds, ever-increasing popularity of equity stock and bonds, growing number of banks turning to capital market activities, banks had to reassess their marketing strategy. A more rigorous pursuit of service quality based on identification of service quality issues and service quality gaps has begun using a variety of techniques, including market research. Financial sector reforms in India have opened up many new areas of operations to the commercial banks especially in the capital market. As a consequence, today we find a good number of Indian commercial banks engaged in management of public issues, loan syndication, private placement, portfolio management, project counseling and corporate counseling. Commercial banks have emerged as important players in the capital market by launching mutual funds. However, at the same time the reform process, easing the entry of private sector in banking and deregulating the interest rate has intensified competition among banks and from non-banking financial intermediaries. In view of increasing ferocity of competition it is high time to put more emphasis on development of a sophisticated marketing strategy to the fullest satisfaction of the customers.

SEARCH FOR A MARKETING STRATEGY

"Catching customer" as the marketing strategy has now become redundant in the context of challenges confronted by the service marketing institutions. However, some institutions are still harbouring with this involving recurring costs and efforts. As this strategy targets a customer for a single transaction and forget after termination of each transaction, which is termed as 'transaction banking', creating new customer needs a continuous and untiring efforts. This may not be possible any more in the present competitive market to create new customers easily. The modern day marketing environment demands a marketing strategy which not only catches customer but also more significantly retain the customer once created. The service institution shall have to resort to a strategy that enabling them to sustain their friendly relation with the customer for years to come. Retention of customer and getting their perennial patronage may be ensured by a marketing strategy called "Relationship banking" which put emphasis on maintaining relationship with the customer. Relationship banking tries to ensure both the revenue growth and cost effectiveness. However, to have a successful "Relationship banking" or whatever marketing strategy, a process with clear vision is necessary. Now, a question comes to mind frequently as to where the marketing strategy starts and with what it will end up? Here, a modest attempt has been made to suss out a strategy for marketing of banking services in the context of present changing environment. The strategy would emphasise on customer satisfaction as the central point with the help of various activities. Different aspects that are included in the strategy have been discussed below:

Market Survey

Although market survey is conventionally used for marketing of physical products, in the present time the

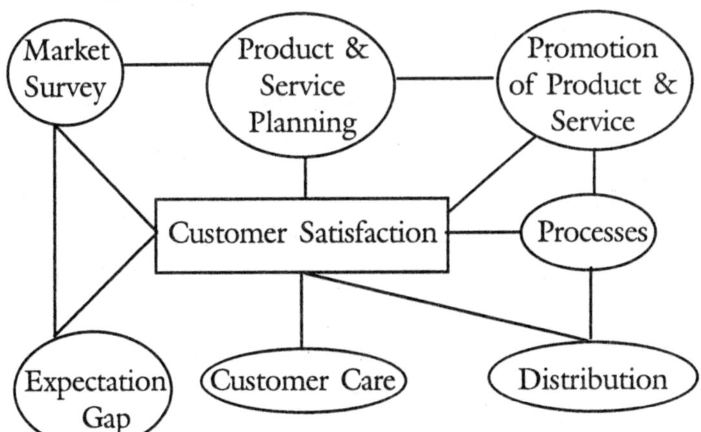

Marketing Strategy—A Model

relevance of market survey in regard to services also has become prominent. Market survey would help the bank to conceive a marketing strategy with a clear vision. It would enable the bank to have a better understanding about potential customers, identifying the target group, identifying needs, wants and demands of the potential as well as existing customers, investigating the difficulties of customers, investigating customer preferences and so on. These information collected through market survey would bring out a design of marketing strategy as well as product ideas to the product planners of banks. Information on socio-economic conditions, banking habit, income level, level of education of the people of a particular area and information regarding geographical condition, existence of other financial institutions and the local economy of the area collected through market survey would enable the bank to have success targets at different level and in different field beforehand.

Product and Service Planning

Product planning in the context of banking, would denote devising schemes and services. On the basis of the processed information collected from market survey banks should develop banking products or services keeping in mind the expectation levels of various groups of customers. Product planning encompasses safety, security, return, flexibility, timing and most importantly benefits. In the present competitive environment two things perhaps would be more relevant in the context of product planning are: (a) to become early bird and (b) to attach additional attributes with product. To become early bird means to come first with the new product idea and to launch the product or services in the market prior to the competitors. Secondly, the product should have some additional benefits than the competitors' product. In this regard Theodore Levitt had suggested four different levels constituting a total product, i.e. (a) core or generic, (b) expected, (c) augmented and (d) potential.

For an investor, safety and return are the core benefits of a scheme, accurate and timety payment of interest and principal is the expected benefit, additional loan facility or flexibility in maturity period to investor would be augmented benefits while giving gifts, conducting lottery, giving club membership, credit card facility to the investors would come under potential benefit.

Additional facilities and features would attract new customer as well as retain existing customer and would make them loyal to the product. While planning the services or product, the customer preference should also be taken care of. Some customer like to have liquidity in their investment while other may look for more return even with substantial amount of risk and some other want to have safe investment. There should be a room for every kind of customer to get in.

Promotion of Product and Services

Like other product the need of the promotion of banking products also has emerged in the recent time. However, banking products or services can not be demonstrated like other manufactured products. For promotion of these products sales campaign has to be organised with audio-visual aids and gifts schemes may be attached with the products to enhance the awareness and attract the customers. Another strategy of promotion of banking products the banks may take up is society friendly works. By sponsoring workshop, tournaments, sports, environmental drive, health camp etc. banks may come closer to the potential customers of the society and may promote the products and services they offer.

Small savings department of government of Assam, as a promotional measure, introduced a Gift Coupon contest in 1999 for the small investors who invested their money in small savings instruments like National Saving Certificate, Kissan Vikas Patra etc. The gift contest contained with may attractive gifts like cars, mobike, scooter, colour television, refrigerator etc. For every Rs. 1000/- investment in the above mentioned instruments a gift coupon was issued. It received a stupendous response of the investors and the department mobilised more than double amount in those instruments compared to the previous year. Still the department is going with the same measure. Under the normative approach suggested by 9th Finance Commission, under which resource mobilised by the State Government towards National Saving instruments is one of the criteria for making devolution resources from the centre to the state. Obviously the resources mobilised through national saving instruments, a share of which comes back to the state to be utilised for the development for the concerned state and state takes initiative for marketing of the instruments. This measure enable the Govt. of Assam to multiply the magnitude of savings.

Processes

Operations and processes of the banks should be made speedy and accurate. They should be technology friendly which is the most important criteria to be the early bird in the present competitive world. Various new technology for example "Any Time Money", Home banking, Internet banking should be made available to the customer as soon as possible. Membership of SWIFT, adoption of WAP technology etc. in order to expedite the transaction worldwide would help the banks to attract customers towards them. In nutshell, whatever new technology emerges which provide smooth and speedy services to the customer should be adopted subject to the demand of the customers.

Distribution

It is high time to re-design the distribution network of banking services. Still many of the banks do not put much effort in distributing services products. Distribution does not only mean authorising certain branches or all branches to offer certain services. In fact, it is the need of the hour that the bank should expand their distribution network by adopting various strategies to catch untapped areas and to retain present areas. Banks should put emphasis on extension of field force that can directly contact the customers for marketing of products and services. As discussed earlier, the relationship banking believes in making relationship rather then making transactions. Personal contact is the most powerful tool in this regard. There cannot be a better opportunity for a bank marketer to influence customer behavior then the face to face interaction afforded by personal selling. Another advantage of personal selling to the marketer is that in this case the marketer can control the proceedings, assess its impact and evaluate its effectiveness instantly.

However, it may not be always feasible to meet all the people face to face in a country with huge population like India. Another distribution strategy has newly emerged called Multi level Marketing can be adopted for extensive network among all the people. Multi-level Marketing is a strategy where products are distributed and marketed by the customer himself or herself. As the customers become marketers here, hence it becomes very easy to expand the channel. In this system when a potential customer purchases certain products, immediately he becomes a distributor of the same products. If any body purchases the products on his advice the former will get a commission on sales proceeds. Besides he will get discount on subsequent purchases of the products by him or any body else on his name. Similarly the second customer will also get commission if somebody becomes a customer on his advice. In this way the chain of distribution goes on a multilevel basis.

For effective distribution of banking products specially non-conventional products (i.e. Mutual funds units, term deposits schemes, capital market links instruments etc.) banks can open more outlet of its own or by appointing channel partners. Recently IDBI has rightly entered into an agreement with the postal department to sell its products through post offices. Banks also can take this strategy to have a wider market for their products even in rural remote areas.

CUSTOMER CARE

Proper attention towards customers would attract the customers to the same bank on perpetual basis. However, in many commercial banks (specially PSU banks) very often it is observed, customers are treated in such a way as if they are coming to the bank for their own interest only. Employees seldom realise the bank's interest involved with customers. What the banks need is the attitudinal change of employees. They should try to come up to level of expectation of the customer with the massage "Never say no to the customer".

Recently a multinational insurance company 'standard life' has started a scheme in Metro cities of India with a special feature that in case the customer meets an accident and hospitalized, a single phone call would be sufficient to receive his claim of the policy, the insurance company's representatives would come to the hospital where the customer is admitted to honour the claims of the customer in regard to medical expenses. Such customer care would attract many more customer towards this scheme.

In fact customer care begins after the sell is over. Sometimes, customers suffer from post purchase anxiety after purchasing a particular product or investing in a scheme. He may be having many questions to clarify. During this period taking care of the customers is very significant and once the bank wins the confidence of a particular customer in this phase it becomes long lasting one. Some times customer may have certain complaint regarding quality of products or service, features of the products or they may have some other preferences. Handling these complaints after selling the product banks can have a service quality audit as well as make a favourable relationship with the customer. Another benefit of customer care for the marketer is that the marketer can do cross selling while handling complaint. The marketer can sell another product which may be preferred much by the customer; not only that, he can make new customer through the existing customer by joint campaign or handling complaint jointly.

EXPECTATION GAP

Each and every customer has a particular level of expectation for the services that he gets from this bank. The bank should ensure that its product and services have been able to discharge utility up to the expected level of satisfaction. Through service quality audit banks should trace out the level of customer satisfaction. Expectation gap is the difference between the expected satisfaction of a customers and the realised satisfaction. A feed back from the customers is necessary in order to identify the level of expectation gap.

The UCO Bank has got housing loan scheme but when a customer approached the branch manager of a branch for a housing loan, he insisted that the instalment repayment has to be made by the employer of the lonee through a separate cheque after deducting it from the salary of the employee (lonee). Many institutions do not have the practice of repaying employees' obligation directly to lending agency by issuing a separate cheque. It also warrants the employer to segregate the employee's salary into two parts one to be paid to the employee and other to the lending bank. This cause inconvenience to the customer to take a loan and here emerges an expectation gap.

Ascertainment of expectation gap would help the banks to develop their product and service in a better way with added features keeping the customers' convenience and preferences in mind. This would enable the bank to bring the customers close and customers also will feel honoured by banks.

EPILOGUE

A strategy which put emphasis on maintaining the relationship with the customer on perpetual basis is the need of the hour in marketing of banking services. The ultimate aim of the strategy would be to transform the customers into advocates and supporters of the services. For that, the customers have to be surved upto their level of expectation. Once customers are satisfied to the fullest extend with the services that a bank provide, they would spontaneously and unknowingly advocate the services and products of the bank. What needed is the frequent and proper customer care. Thus, the new regime demand a never ending marketing strategy which would target not to make new customers always but to retain all the customers with the attainment of customers satisfaction.

REFERENCES

1. Chand, Nirakar (1999), "Relationship Management—A strategic Approach", *SBI Monthly Review,* April.
2. Kumar, L.N.(1999), *Strategic Marketing of Banking Services,* Suneja Publisher, New Delhi.
3. Payne, Adrian (1998), *The Essence Service Marketing,* Prentice Hall of India, New Delhi.
4. Rao, Prasada P.S.(1996, 'Relationship Banking as a Competitive Strategy', *SBI Monthly Review,* July.

6

STRATEGIES FOR BANK MARKETING: A STUDY OF SBI

—BASUDEV CHHATOI & UMESH C. PATNAIK

Marketing strategy implies development of an action plan to achieve the marketing objectives. Just highlighting marketing in the cozy atmosphere of high offices and issuing directives to subordinate offices emphasizing its importance does not serve the purpose. It involves skill and concerted effort on the part of the management to evolve tools and techniques, which are understood and accepted throughout the organization in furtherance of the marketing cause.

According to Granroos, marketing strategy in the case of services may consist in (*i*) Traditional External Marketing (*ii*) Internal Marketing (*iii*) Interactive Marketing. Traditional external marketing consists of usual four 'Ps' of Product, Price, Place, and Promotion of Marketing mix. Internal marketing implies that the service firm must effectively train and motivate its customer-contact-employees as well as all the supporting service personnel to work as a team to provide customer satisfaction. Interactive marketing emphasizes that the perceived service quality is highly dependent on the quality of buyer/seller interaction. It describes the skill of employees in handling customer contact and covers delivery of the product in a most satisfying manner.

On the backdrop of the above concept the present paper attempts to study the marketing strategies adopted by the State Bank of India (hereafter referred to as 'the Bank') on the presumption that if the marketing mix is perfect, employees are able and willing and they get the required organizational support, then interactive marketing which is the culminating factor of marketing effort is a natural outcome.

TRADITIONAL MARKETING

Traditional marketing which refers to the marketing mix is a combination of tools and techniques with which a marketer has to meet the customer in furthering his marketing objectives. The tools, as propounded by different authorities, are many. But traditionally, they are the famous 4Ps, viz, Product, Price, Place, Promotion. Marketing executive is a "Mixer of Ingredients". He is constantly engaged in fashioning creatively a mix of marketing procedures and policies in his effort to produce a profitable enterprise. It is needless to state that all products and services are not for all segments, all segments may not afford the same price, the same place may not be suitable for all segments for delivery of the product/service or the same promotional measure may not arouse same level of confidence in all customers. Therefore, the essence of traditional marketing lies in providing each customer segment with a cost effective mix of 4Ps that most suits its needs.

PRODUCT

A product is anything that can be offered to a market for attention, use or consumption that might satisfy a want or need. It includes physical objects, services, persons, places, organization and ideas. The function of marketing is to assess what attributes the consumer seeks from the product and to combine these to make the most attractive product, offering which, in turn, will optimize the company's profit. Our concern here is with the 'services'. This is the product which banks deal in. 'Service' has its own peculiarities like intangibility, inseparability, variability and perishability. By buying a service a customer does not possess any thing as in case of physical products. What he gets is satisfaction of his wants and needs from the use of the service. Thus a bank product is anything that has the capacity to provide the satisfaction use and return desired by the customer. As Theodore Levitt has suggested, there are four different levels of satisfaction-core, expected, augmented and potential-constituting a total product concept. The basic utility that a customer derives from a product is the core level (the first level) and gradually it transcends into higher levels with more value addition. Thus it becomes essential to keep in mind the idiosyncrasies of a banking product before we frame a product strategy.

Liberalisation has ushered in a competitive era. Competition supplemented by technological development is bringing about revolutionary changes in the banking industry. The traditional products like deposit and advances, because of dwindling spread, are giving way to non-fund based products. As a result, there is a spurt in fee-based income of the banks and diversification of banking business into areas, which were previously not coming under the purview of banking activities. Gold banking, Credit Cards, Project finance, depository services, securitisation, investment banking, and insurance etc. are becoming the order of the day. It is observed that to stay competitive, the Bank has diversified its business and introduced innovative products.

The Bank has a Product Development Group under Personal and Service Department at Central office. It is involved in developing and marketing products/services for the personal segment which is the most sensitive area and

Fig. 1

Product Development Framework at SBI

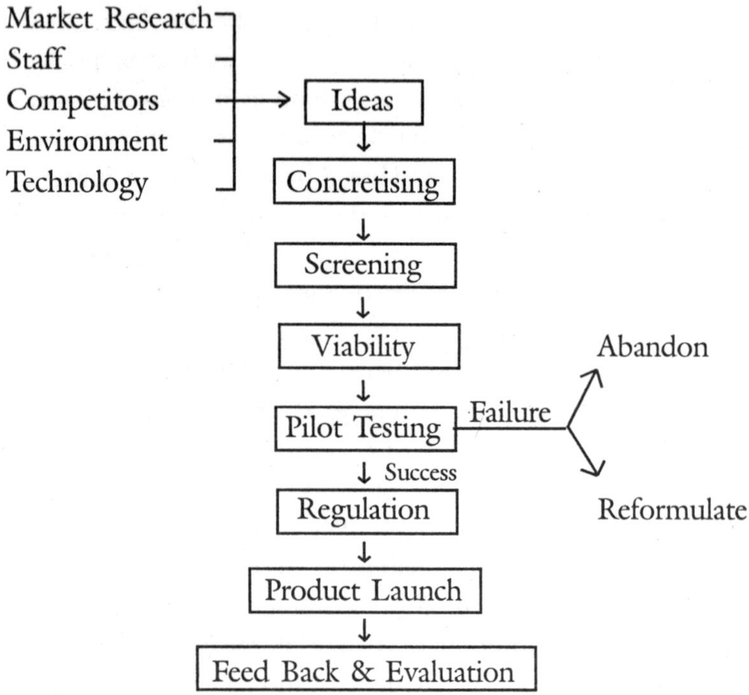

Source: "Vichaar", State Bank Staff College, Gurgaon, July-Sep. 1996, p. 41.

needs variety. The product development process (Fig-1) in the Bank is more or less based on the theoretical framework given by Philip Kotler. Though the procedure has a scientific basis and its products are at par with its competitors, it is observed that some products are not doing well. No doubt, introduction of new products and withdrawal of obsolete ones indicate to the active product policy of the Bank, but some products which are a great success with other banks and not so with the Bank point to inability of the Bank in Marketing of those products.

Table 1

Deposit mobilisation by SBI and All Scheduled Commercial Banks During 1991-98 *(Rs. in Crore)*

Year	*SBI*		*ASCBs*		*Share of SBI*
	Dep.	*Growth*	*Dep.*	*Growth*	
1991	48374	11.17	200568	16.67	24.12
1992	60192	24.43	237107	18.22	25.39
1993	66317	10.18	275851	16.34	24.04
1994	76406	15.21	323977	17.45	23.58
1995	85122	11.41	379174	17.04	22.45
1996	96395	13.24	426073	12.37	22.62
1997	110701	14.84	492227	15.53	22.49
1998	131091	18.42	592068	20.28	22.14
AARG		15.00		16.80	

Note: AARG - Average Annual Rate of Growth.

Source:
1. Banking Statistics, Basic Statistical Return of RBI. (1972-1995)
2. Quarterly handouts of RBI March 1996, 97 & 98.
3. Annual Reports of SBI.

Table 1 indicates that in the post liberalization period deposits of the Bank has grown at an average annual rate of 15 per cent compared to 16.8 per cent that of ASCBs and its market share has gone down from around *25* per cent to 22 percent. Similarly, table-2 indicates that during the same period advances of the Bank has grown at an average annual rate of 11.5 per cent compared to 15.5 per cent that of ASCBs and its market share has gone down from around 33 per cent to 22 per cent. This clearly highlights the fact that the Bank has been exposed to fierce competition from its competitors and needs emphasis on aggressive marketing, at least, to maintain its market position. The bank has the option to exploit the profitable personal segment in the rural and semi urban areas where the competition is less severe and the Bank has the necessary infrastructure.

Table 2

Advances by SBI and all Scheduled Commercial Banks During 1991-98 *(Rs. in Crore)*

Year	*SBI*		*ASCBs*		*Share of CBI*
	Adv.	*Growth*	*Adv*	*Growth*	
1991	40438	17.21	124203	19.07	32.56
1992	44344	09.06	136706	10.07	32.44
1993	47695	07.56	162467	18.84	29.36
1994	41498	(-) 12.99	175891	08.26	23.59
1995	48530	16.995	210939	19.93	23.01
1996	59826	23.27	263533	24.93	22.70
1997	62233	04.02	282237	07.10	22.05
1998	74237	19.29	328637	16.44	22.59
AARG		11.50		15.50	

Note: AARG - Average Annual Rate of Growth.

Source :
1. Banking Statistics, Basic Statistical Return of RBI.
2. Quarterly handouts of RBI March 1996, 97, 98.
3. Annual Reports of SBI.

PRICE

The second 'P' of the marketing mix is price. Price refers to the amount of money a customer is willing to pay for the product. From the supplier's angle, it is the amount of money at which the firm is prepared to offer its goods/services. The seller looks to the cost plus profit and buyer looks to the satisfaction in return for price to be paid. The satisfaction is a judgement, a notion, a feeling and as such cannot be quantified in terms of money. It differs from person to person. Thus, the banks while pricing their products must take care of this factor and rely on product quality and promotion.

Prior to deregulation banks were operating in an administered price regime. RBI was determining the rates of interest on deposits and loans and advances. The charges on subsidiary services were fixed by IBA, which were being implemented under uniform schedule of charges, and banks were given freedom to stipulate the rate schedule in respect of the services, which were not included in the uniform schedule. But, since 1991, with the onset of financial sector reforms, interest rates were deregulated making the pricing of products a challenging job for the banks. Thus pricing which was of little relevance in administered price regime assumed greater importance in the deregulated era from the marketing point of view.

Table-3 shows the fluctuation of interest rates on domestic deposits and State Bank Advance Rate (SBAR) during the post-liberalization period. It is observed that the maximum deposit rate was 13 per cent in 1991. It came down to 9.0 per cent by 1995. Rose again to 13 per cent in 1996 and

Table 3

Interest on Domestic Deposits of SBI

(Per cent Per Annum)

Category of deposits	*With effect from..*				
	9/10/91	*21/1/95*	*16/7/96*	*1/11/97*	*5/3/01*
SB A/C	5	4.5	4.5	4.5	4
30 days up to 45 days	....	....	8	5.0	5.25*
46 days up to 179 days	11	8	9	5.0	6.50
180 days less than 1 year	11	8	10	7.5	7.0
1 year – less than 2 years	12	10	11	10.0	8.5
2 years – less than 3 years	12	9.5	12	10.5	9.0
3 years and above	13	9.0	13	11.5	9.5

Note * 15 days up to 45 days.

Source: BOD/P& SB/CFO/CSL Circulars of SBI.

again came down to 9.5 per cent in 2001. Its comparison with SBAR clearly brings out the rate was among the banks. Finer rates were quoted leading to reduction in the spread. On 9th October 1991 the maximum term deposit rate was 13 per cent and the minimum lending rate (SBAR) was 20 per cent. The spread available to the Bank was 7 per cent. But, by Ist November 1997, the spread was reduced to 1.5 per cent. But the fact is that quoting of finer rate was not based on a scientific costing system. They are market driven. Though it is a sudden death for weaker banks, stronger banks may not sustain it in the long run.

Prior to deregulation the service charges fixed by IBA were hardly related to cost of service to a particular bank and more particularly to a specific activity. In the latter part of 1997, the Bank increased these rates by 30 to 40 per cent on the ground that there was all round escalation in cost and foreign banks were selling their services successfully charging them at higher rates. But the bank has neither any activity wise cost data to justify the escalation nor any reputation of rendering efficient services as foreign banks. Any price rise must accompany increase in quality to be acceptable to the customer. It is high time, the Bank goes for quality database and be cost conscious. It must be noted that any price hike is acceptable to the customer if it is properly explained to him.

PLACE

The third 'P' in marketing mix is place or physical distribution. The very objective of distribution is to get the right product at the right place and at the right time and at the least cost. Hence distribution involves establishment of a strategy covering channels of distribution and physical distribution of the product from the point of production to the point of consumption at a profit. In the banking context, where production and delivery of product/service takes place

Table 4

Branch Expansion of SBI since its Inception

Period	*Branches added during the period*	*No. of branches at the end of the Period*	*Average Annual Addition*
1955	.....	497	.....
1955—1969	1176	1673	84
1969—1990	6749	8422	321
1990—2000	628	9050	63

Source: 1. Everlatest in Banking, SBI Officers' Association, Bhopal.
2. Annual Reports of SBI.

at the same time, distribution requires establishment and functioning of a network of branches through which banking services are delivered.

From the customers' angle, it is the proximity and convenience of operation, which plays a vital role in the selection of a bank, as their need for banking services is repetitive in nature. Thus suitable location, proper layout and provision of facilities for the customers are the key factors to get majority of customers. As it is reflected in Table 4, by the year 2000, the bank with 9050 branches has the distinction of having largest network of branches among all the banks in the world and has been able to become nearer to the customer.

The place is more than a physical place. It is where actual transaction takes place. Thus, the Technological advancement, which has led to telephone banking and Net banking, has rendered the concept of broad based branch network obsolete. In the pursuit of the policy of reaching out to the masses the Bank has ended up with large number of loss making branches. The imposition of capital adequacy norms and prudential accounting standards and fierce competition due to liberalization have further aggravated the situation. Technology which increased the capacity of a branch in handling more business and in its reach forced banks to bring about a change in the branch expansion strategy which is reflected in the slow growth in the number of branch of the Bank during nineties (Table-4). But the Bank has an option left for it. It can utilize its widespread network of branches to increase its business in the rural and semi-urban areas where there is hardly any competition from foreign and new private banks.

PROMOTION

Promotion is a process of persuasive communication and constitutes one of the 4Ps of marketing mix. It relates to the task of informing the target market about the nature and type of firm's product and services, their unique benefits, uses, features as well as price and place at which those would be available. Promotion comprises of four major elements, viz.

Table 5

Expenses incurred on Advertising and Publicity by SBI During 1990-91 and 1999-00

(Rs. in Crore)

Year	*Expenses on Adv. and Pub*	*As a percentage of net profit*
1990 – 91	7.20	6.73
1991 – 92	8.90	5.09
1992 – 93	5.49	2.59
1993 – 94	12.67	4.61
1994 – 95	9.33	1.30
1995 – 96	13.87	1.67
1996 – 97	11.87	0.88
1997 – 98	15.02	0.80
1998 – 99	22.20	2.16
1999 – 00	17.56	0.86

Source: Annual Reports of SBI.

Advertising, Publicity, Sales Promotion and Personal selling. To achieve the objectives of promotion all the four are used to some degree. Selection of the mix is based on their relative strength. Thus, the promotional mix vary from time to time and place to place depending upon the major customer segment and the type of service offered.

SBI has been giving advertisement, and publicity to its products/services when there is a need for it. Particularly, when a new product is launched, the bank goes for it in large scale. The various ways in which the Bank does it are advertisement through press, hoardings, pamphlets, posters, road shows, souvenir, press conferences, radio, TV, and personal selling etc. Table-5 shows the amount of money the Bank has spent on advertising and publicity during the post-liberalization period. In this period, though there is a rise in the amount of expenditure in absolute terms, there is a perceptible decline when it is observed in relation to the net profit of the Bank.

INTERNAL MARKETING

The concept of internal marketing as propounded by Prof. Leonard L. Berry, presumes the bank employees as its internal customers and jobs offered to them as products. So effort should be made to offer a product mix that satisfies the need and wants of these internal customers. The same marketing tools which are used to attract and retain customers (external) can gainfully be employed to attract, retain and inspire the employees (internal customers), particularly the best among them. People are the living, thinking and feeling beings that constitute the internal customers. Therefore, it requires a carefully planned systematic approach for procuring, developing and managing the workforce.

In a banking concern where product differential is hard to maintain and price differential is almost nil, the only area where a distinctiveness can be maintained is the quality of human resources. Banks provide service. Services by their nature are inseparable from the provider. In this context the bank employees who provide these services assume paramount importance. How far and to what extent the quality level of their performance will reach is solely left to the employees concerned. As a satisfied employee can deliver total satisfaction to a customer it becomes important for banks to satisfy the needs and wants of the employees on priority basis.

Table 6

Expenses incurred by SBI on training during 19996 – 98

Rs: 000

Year	*Expenses on Training*	*As a percentage of profits*
1995-96	279852	3.36
1996-97	338632	2.55
1997-98	421401	2.26

Source: LHO Bhubaneswar (Orissa)

The Bank realizes that human resources management as a key area which will provide it the needed cutting edge in its endeavour towards competitive excellence. So it has a clear cut HRD mission which recognizes its employees as a member of an effective team and State Bank community where from each member should derive motivation to activate his potential to contribute to the achievement of bank's goal and derive satisfaction there from. The Human Resources Committee in the corporate office formulates various personnel policies in order to bring about an integrated management perspective. To keep pace with the changing environment, the bank has been making continuous effort to enhance knowledge, develop skills and reorient attitude of the employees. The Bank has 53 staff training centers, 2 apex level colleges and 2 institutes. Besides in-house training provided by STCs, the colleges conduct research on relevant topics. The Bank has a Visiting Faculty Scheme to make the training system more effective. Table 6 gives the figures relating to the expenses incurred by the bank on training of its employees. It could be seen that the expenses in absolute terms have been increasing from year to year but when compared to net profit, it reflects a downward trend. Besides training, the Bank has a good promotional system. It provides a lot of amenities to its employees. It also has various schemes for the welfare of its staff.

The analysis of internal marketing of the Bank reveals that though the Bank has rightly taken necessary steps and formulated various plans and programmes to developed its work force, the hard fact is that HRD has remained a grey area for the Bank. This is the area which needs focussed attention and concerted effort to make the Bank World class.

INTERACTIVE MARKETING

Quality of service is dependent on the quality of buyer/ seller interaction. This is the point, which may lead to creation of a customer or not. Though we may win him at that point of time, because of some reason or other, we may not be able to retain him if interaction at that point is not satisfying enough to leave a lasting impact on him. We may have a beautiful marketing mix of traditional 4Ps which brings the customers to us, our internal marketing may be well enough to prepare a band of able and willing work force, but if we fail at this point, all our effort so far will be futile. This is the reason which makes interactive marketing so important.

As given in the fig-2, interactive marketing involves the able and willing employees at one end and the customer

Fig - 2

Interactive Marketing

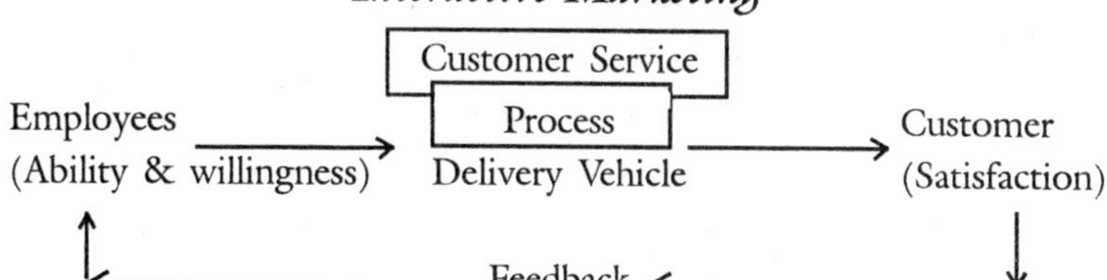

whose needs are to be satisfied at the other. They are linked by the process, the delivery vehicle which is to be handled as delicately as possible to leave a lasting impact on the customer. While doing so, the customer-contact employee takes care to learn and mend his action according to the feedback received from the customer.

As it is observed, systems and procedures in vogue in the Bank for delivery of customer satisfying needs are not up to mark and needs attention. They have not kept pace with the changing environment and changing demands. Though the Bank claims to have implemented most of the recommendations of various committees on customer service, criticism of Bank's poor customer service still continues. Strict observance of rules, multiplicity of returns, duplicity of efforts have added to the work load of the staff leaving very little time for them for paying due attention to customers' needs.

CONCLUSION

In this world of rapidly self outdating technological advancement, when multi-channel banking is giving way to cross-channel banking, and a credit card, drawing cash from an ATM or verifying savings account balance over a phone or Net no more excite customers, framing of marketing strategies has become a real tough job for the bank marketers. Each time, he has to come out with a new formula to meet the ever-growing expectation of the customers. Thus, in the given scenario, the bank, which is able to convert the emerging threats into opportunities, is going to be a real winner. As it is observed, the SBI has most of the requirements of a good bank. But, if its internal customers come out of the cocoon of unionism, feel themselves as members of the State Bank family and make the interactive marketing a real success, days are not far, when the Bank is counted among the great banks of the World.

REFERENCES

1. David, J.L. and Ferrell, D.C., *Marketing Strategy and Plans,* Prentice Hall of India, New Delhi, 1982.
2. Ghoshroy, D., *Bank Marketing a Hand Book for Branch Bankers,* BDP Publishers, Pune, 1994.
3. Kotler, Philip, *Principles of Marketing,* Prentice Hall of India Pvt Ltd, New Delhi, 1983.
4. Litter, Dale, *Marketing and Product Development,* Heritage Publishers, New Delhi, 1985.
5. Madhukar, R.K., *Dynamics of Bank Marketing,* Sri Sudhindra Publishing House, Bangalore, 1990.
6. Murry, Keith, B., "A test of Services Marketing theory; Consumer Information Acquisition Activities", *Journal of Marketing,* Jan. 1991.
7. Neil, H.Borden, "The Concept of Marketing Mixs", *Journal of Advertising Research,* Vol. 14, June 1964, Advertising Research Foundation, USA.
8. Ogden Ross, W., *Marketing in Commercial Banks: How to Proceed,* Master Co. Press Inc., Michigan, 1968.
9. Peter, D.B, *Marketing,* McGraw Hill Inc. USA, 1988.
10. Saxena, K. K. *Bank Marketing: Concepts and Appplications,* Skylark Publications, New Delhi, 1988.

7

CUSTOMER SATISFACTION IN BANKING SECTOR

—SANDEEP TANDON

Technology, people and customers are the three elements on which hinges the success of banking in the fast changing economic environment. The ultimate performance of a bank depends upon the satisfaction of its customers. In the emerging competitive and technological driven banking era, banks have to strive hard for retaining and enlarging their customer base. Now banking activities are not confined to borrowing (collection of savings) and lending (disbursement of loans), but provide a plethora of services keeping in mind the requirements and convenience of customers. In response to the new technological challenges, organisation have to involve internal capabilities and skilled human resource management which is fundamental in generating these capabilities. (Mittal and Kumra 2001).

Customer satisfaction largely depends on the extent to which their needs and expectation are being fulfilled. Customers have various expectations for banks to consider. Some of the expectations relate to the quality of the bank personnel. Some may relate to the place where the bank is rendering the services and some to the process i.e. the sequence and the flow of services involved in their rendering.

CUSTOMER-RELATIONSHIP BANKING

The banks that do well in 1990s and 2000 AD will be those which rediscover the customer through the cutting edge known as relationship banking. Bank marketing is concerned with the exchange relationship between the bank and its customers where customer service and quality are the key linkages of such relationship. In the 1990s the banking industry took a turn towards liberalisation, privatisation and globalisation exposing them to unprecedented competition for which banks found a solution in the strategy of 'Relationship Banking' [B.L.Vaisnav 2000].

Customer Relationship management is a well defined series of functions, skills, processes and technologies which altogether allow organisations to more profitably manage and satisfy customers as tangible assets. The concept of customer relationship management when seen in the context of e-business or transactions over an electronic medium, it translates it into e-customer relationship management which essentially deals with managing customer interactions over the web.

Following are some of the latest e-customer relationship management techniques used by banks to improve the level of its customers satisfaction:

1. **Internet Banking:-** Internet is being used by banks to disseminate information to customers about banks products and services through their websites.
2. **ATMS:-** Until now ATM services have been confined to deposits and withdrawals from bank accounts by customers. At present number of ATMS functioning in our country is 1800, which is likely to increase upto 4000 by next year.
3. **E.Mail:-** This is considered to be the best and cheapest means of communication through which banks inform their customers about bank's services.
4. **Customer Smart Cards:-** These cards are issued

to key customers. Smart cards carry all the relevant information of various purchases, to recall customers to keep a track of purchase trends.

Objectives and Methodology

In view of the above, the present study is carried out with the following objectives:-

1. To study the actual level of customer satisfaction in four commercial banks i.e. State Bank of India (SBI), Punjab National Bank (PNB), Central Bank of India (CBI) and Jammu and Kashmir Bank Ltd. (JKB) by analysing their attitude towards following variables:
   a) Bank
   b) Employees
   c) Management.
2. To make a comparative analysis of level of customers satisfaction in four banks.

The present study is based on the survey carried out in Jammu city. 111 customers with the aforementioned banks were selected on the basis of stratified random sampling method. The sample constitutes 10% of the total number of employees of Bank in Jammu city. Data was collected through a well-drafted and pretested questionnaire structured on five point (5<------>1) Likert scale administered personally to the respondents.

Customers have been split up in three categories i.e. Businessmen, Service class and practitioners (Doctors, Lawyers, Chartered Accountants) for judging their level of satisfaction towards the aforesaid three variables.

The break up of the sample of 111 respondents having accounts with the selected commercial banks is as follows:-

State Bank of India	33

Punjab National Bank	:-	26
Central Bank of India	:-	20
Jammu & Kashmir Bank Ltd.	:-	32

FINDIGS

Customers Satisfaction in State Bank of India

Table 1 shows that a total of 33 customers of the bank have reported overall highest satisfaction which is evident from the mean score of 3.20, which is above average out of these, service class is the highest satisfied lot (3.47) while Businessmen have put up the lowest mean score (2.86). It falls in the below average range. Practitioners seem to be moderately satisfied as they are showing mean score of 3.27. Table further shows that mean scores of service class, customers and practitioners are higher than the overall average of the bank.

Comparative analysis of the three variables for the study show that customers are showing good response towards management of the bank which is clear from the mean score of 3.22, which is higher than those of other two variables i.e. Attitude towards Bank (3.20) and attitude towards Employees (3.17). Thus table makes it clear that staff of the bank has not been able to make customers happy with their behaviour. That is why table is showing the lowest mean score (3.17) regarding this particular variable.

A comparative analysis of overall mean score and actual mean of different variables shows that regarding customers attitude towards Bank, mean score of service class (3.43) and Practitioners (3.26) are higher than overall average. Mean score of 2.91 is lower than the overall mean score.

Table 1

Customers Satisfaction in Banks
State Bank of India

Number of Customers	*Variable-I Attitude towards Bank*	*Variable-II Attitude Towards Employees*	*Variable-III Attitude towards Management*	*Average Mean score*
*B11	2.91	2.61	3.04	2.86
*S11	3.43	3.55	3.42	3.47
*P11	3.26	3.35	3.19	3.27
Average Mean score	3.20	3.17	3.22	3.20

B- Businessmen.
S-Service Class
P-Practitioners.

As regards second variable i.e. attitude towards Employees except businessmen (2.61), other two categories of customers have responded well i.e. 3.35 of service class and 3.35 of practitioners.

Customers have reported highest score of 3.22 towards management of the bank. It is also higher than actual average of Businessmen (3.04) and practitioners (3.19). To sum up, it may be stated Businessmen, though having the frequent dealings with the bank, still is the least satisfied lot especially with the behaviour of employees.

Customers Satisfaction in Punjab National Bank

An overall mean score of 3.06 has been shown in the table 2. Comparing the actual responses with the overall response, it may be stated that it is lower than those of service class customers (3.33) and practitioners (3.14). Conversely, it is higher than that of businessmen (2.71).

A comparative analysis of overall averages with the actual mean score, table under reference shows that overall mean score (3.05) is lower than averages for service class (3.32) and practitioners (3.23) but higher than that of business class (2.60), so far as attitude of employees towards Bank is concerned.

Table 2

Customers Satisfaction in Punjab National Bank

Number of customers	*Variable-I Attitude towards Bank*	*Variable-II Attitude towards Employees*	*Variable-III Attitude towards Management*	*Average Mean Score*
B	2.60	2.52	3.01	2.71
S	3.32	3.45	3.21	3.33
P	3.23	3.04	3.16	3.14
Average Mean Score	3.05	3.00	3.13	3.06

Customers do not seem happy with the staff of the Bank which is clear from the mean score of 3.00, which is just average. It is again higher than that of Businessmen responses (2.52) while it is lower than those of service class (3.45) and Practitioners (3.04). Highest degree of satisfaction has been shown towards management of the bank (3.13) which is lower than those of service class and practitioners i.e. 3.21 and 3.16 respectively, but higher than of businessmen (3.01).

Customers Satisfaction in Central Bank of India

Table 3 signifies almost similar position as that of two banks discussed above. Though Central Bank is a small bank, still its customers are most satisfied i.e. 3.30. This, when compared to actual averages shown by different categories of customers, it becomes clear from the table under reference that it is higher than those of businessmen responses (3.04) and Practitioners (3.19) but lower than that of service class (3.67).

Table further shows that comparing the variable-wise position of the bank regarding Ist variable i.e. attitude towards Bank, overall average (3.31) is higher than that of businessmen and practitioners (3.18) and (3.25) respectively while lower than service class as lower (3.51). It clarifies the fact that Businessmen and Practitioners are not satisfied with the Bank. Same is the position regarding variable attitude towards management i.e. (3.31).

As regards third category i.e. attitude towards management, overall mean is lower than that of service class customers (3.96) and higher than in case of practitioners (3.04) very poor response has been shown by businessmen as clear from the below average mean score of 2.92 second variable i.e. attitude towards employees shows lowest mean score of 3.28 which is lower than that of service class customers (3.55) but higher than that of businessmen (3.01). It is equal to that of practitioners (3.28).

Table 3

Customers Satisfaction in Central Bank of India

Number of Customers	*Varaible-I Attitude towards Bank*	*Variable-II Attitude towards Management*	*Variable-III Attitude towards Management*	*Average Mean Score*
B8	3.18	3.01	2.92	3.04
S6	3.51	3.55	3.96	3.67
P6	3.25	3.28	3.04	3.19
Average Mean Score	3.31	3.28	3.31	3.30

Customers Satisfaction in Jammu & Kashmir Bank Ltd.

The position of Jammu and Kashmir Bank Ltd. is different from other banks so far as mean score of practitioners is concerned. Their mean score has been estimated at 2.90 which is below average range. Lowest overall mean score of 3.01 has been worked out against which mean score of service class customers is the highest (3.41) as compared to Businessmen (2.71) and Practitioners (2.90) as shown in table-4.

Table 4

Customer Satisfaction in Jammu Kashmir Bank Ltd.

Number of Customers	*Variable-I Attitude towards Bank*	*Variable-II Attitude towards Management*	*Variable-III Attitude towards Management*	*Average Mean Score*
B12	2.93	2.75	2.44	2.71
S10	3.45	3.01	3.78	3.41
P10	3.11	2.87	2.71	2.90
Av. Mean Score	3.16	2.88	3.03	3.01

Comparative analysis of the actual mean score of customers with the overall mean scores, variable-wise, reveals that the highest degree of satisfaction lies in case of their attitude towards Bank (3.16). As against this overall average, mean scores of business class customers (2.93) and Practitioners (2.71). Customers responses regarding employees are very poor as is evident from the mean score of 2.88 which is lower than that of majority of service class customers (3.01) employees show dissatisfaction towards Bank.

Table 5

Customers' Satisfaction in Four Commercial Banks : A comparative analysis between 3 Variables.

Bank	*Variable-I (Attitude towards Bank)*	*Variable-II (Attitude towards Employees)*	*Variable-III (Attitude towards Management)*	*Average Mean Score*
SBI	3.20	3.17	3.22	3.20
PNB	3.05	3.00	3.13	3.06
CBI	3.31	3.28	3.31	3.30
J&K	3.16	2.88	3.03	3.01
Average Mean Score	3.18	3.08	3.17	3.14

Above table shows the customer's satisfaction in all the four commercial banks through judging their attitude towards three variables viz. Attitude towards Bank, attitude towards employees and attitude towards management.

Comparative analysis of the level of customers satisfaction in four banks shows that overall average mean score has been estimated at 3.14 which is little above average. This shows that the customers are not fully satisfied with the services offered by the banks. On comparing it with the actual mean scores of four Banks, table shows that customers of Central Bank of India have shown a highest level of satisfaction i.e. 3.30 whereas State Bank of India has been ranked second in order of satisfaction amongst customers. Customers of Punjab National Bank and Jammu and Kashmir Bank Ltd. are showing almost same mean score i.e. 3.06 and 3.01 respectively which is lower than the overall average mean score. It shows the dissatisfaction is prevailing in these two banks. Though Central Bank of India, being a bank with few number of branches is having good relations with its customers. Likewise other three

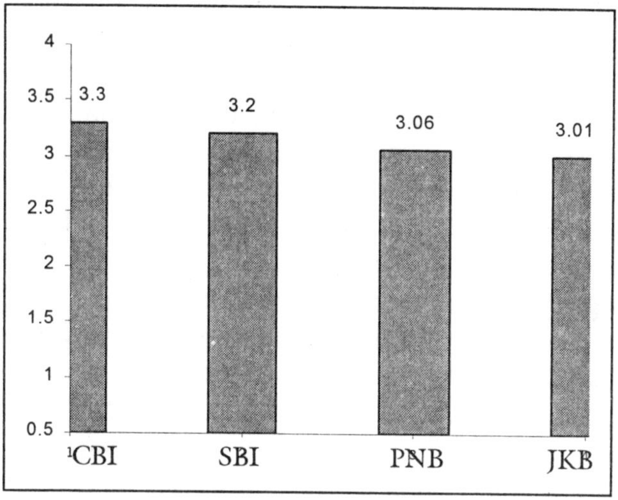

banks should also try to raise the level of customers satisfaction by providing maximum facilities to them.

A cursory glance of the graph depicts the overall comparison of level of customer satisfication in commercial banks. Customers of Central Bank of India seem to be the happiest lot. The average of average mean score of same has been worked out at 3.30 which is little above average. Regarding other three banks, it may be stated that satisfaction level of customers of State Bank of India is lower than that of CBI which has been estimated at an average of 3.20. This is followed by Punjab National Bank and Jammu & Kashmir Bank Ltd at an average of 3.06 and 3.01 respectively.

Above discussion leads to the conclusion that customer satisfaction of all banks is falling within the range of 3.00 to 3.50. Central Bank of India (being a bank with less number of branches) is still most satisfied.

SUGGESTIONS

To improve the level of customers satisfaction few suggestions are made. Bank personnel should be willing and ready to serve the customers during working hours of the bank. They should be quick and prompt in offering the services. Employees working in the banking institution should be knowledgeable and skilful and the same should be reflected in their behaviour. Apart from this, customer service should have consistent quality. All the risks and side effects if any, should be conveyed to the customers. Banks should be conveniently located and physical facilities should be attractive. Employees should be properly equipped with communication facilities for easy access and they should be polite, respectful, flexible, friendly and accommodating with customers.

On the whole, the aforementioned suggestions, if implemented would go a long way in improving the level of customer satisfaction in Banking sector.

Following items were selected pertaining to various aspects for evaluating the level of customers satisfaction in banking sector:

VARIABLE I:- ATTITUDE OF CUSTOMERS TOWARDS BANK

S.No.

1. You opened an account in the Bank because it is easily approachable.
2. You opened an account in the Bank because it is reputed bank.
3. You opened an account in the Bank because the bank was primarily recommended by one of your freinds / relatives.
4. The Bank does not consume much time in opening of an account.
5. You feel satisfied with the maintenance, operation and safety of the account by the Bank.
6. The Bank takes care of your interests.

7. The Bank values your suggestions.
8. You feel satisfied with the fixed account services of the Bank.
9. You feel satisfied with the current account services of the Bank.
10. You feel satisfied with the recurring deposit services of the Bank.
11. The Bank takes more time in extending overdraft facility.
12. The Bank adopts a liberal attitude towards overdraft facility.
13. Overdraft facility requires many formalities to be fulfilled by the customers.
14. The discounting of bills facility is done easily.
15. In case due to delay in discounting of bills on the part of bank, the bank duly, compensates you for the loss of interest.
16. The locker services are easily available in the bank.
17. The bank provides proper services to customers having lockers.
18. The foreign exchange service is easily available.
19. The foreign exchange service is much time consuming.
20. The bank takes lesser time in giving short term loans.
21. The Bank takes less time in giving long term loans.

VARIABLE II:- ATTITUDE OF CUSTOMERS TOWARDS EMPLOYEES

22. Employees are helpful and cooperative.
23. They are courteous and well behaved.
24. They immediately attend you at counters.
25. They guide you properly in case of any problem faced in fulfilling the formalities.

26. The employees feed you with approriate information required by you.
27. Employees maintain your pass books upto date and correctly.
28. Employees maintain punctuality in Bank timings.
29. You feel happy by interacting with employees.
30. They reply to your questions politely.
31. They are indifferent and callous towards you.
32. Employees are sufficiently intelligent to perform their jobs.
33. Employees are conscious of their work and responsibility.
34. Employees indulge gossipping during working hours.

VARIABLE III:- ATTITUDE OF CUSTOMERS TOWARDS MANAGEMENT

35. The Management has liberal policies regarding:-
    i) Discounting of bills.
    ii) Overdraft Facilities.
    iii) Cash Credit Facilities.
    iv) Locker services.
    v) Short term loans.
    vi) Long term loans.
36. Your grievances are properly redressed by the management.
37. The Management of the bank is effective in getting their targets realised through its employees.
38. The Managers are very cooperative.
39. The Managers know their jobs well.
40. The Managers easily extend financial assistance to rich and influencial persons.
41. Managers avoid customers.

42. Money is shelled out of your pocket to get loans sanctioned by the Bank.
43. Managers always exort their employees to be careful about the interest of customers.

REFERENCES

1. Mittal R.K. and Kumra Rajeev, 'E-CRM in Indian Bank: An overviews', *Delhi Business Review,* Vol. 2, No. 1, p. 73, Jan - June 2001.
2. Tandon, Sandeep, *Organisational Behaviour of Banking Sector in India,* Mohit Publications, 2001.
3. Vaishnav, B.L. 'Service Marketing: Global Perspectives'. *The Indian Journal of Commerce,* Vol. 53. No. 3, p. 27, July - Sept 2000.

8

DFIs IN TRANSITION— THE INDIAN EXPERIENCE

—A. P. PATI

The financial sector in India is in the midst of important structural changes. The initiation of reform process since early nineties has brought competition into force. The liberalisation-privatisation - globalisation combination has transformed the protected economy into a more vibrant, open and dynamic one. The metamorphosis has shown better prospects for growth rate through new opportunities, but side by side it has posed formidable challenges to the different constituents of financial system. The competitiveness in the financial system has put pressure on financial institutions to adopt and innovate. And as a major constituent of financial system the development banks, popularly known as development financial institutions (DFIs) have also experienced lot of changes. Further, the impact of the change on DFIs has been magnified by the globalisation of international financial markets, and by radical changes in information technology. These changes have made far-reaching impact on different functional aspects of DFIs; like resource mobilisation, product diversification, business strategy, disclosure norms etc. DFIs have started reorienting their operational goals and strategies to meet these challenges.

Considering the above transformations, in this article an attempt has been made to examine the impact of on going reform process on DFIs and how they have responded to these changes. In this article DFIs mean industrial DFIs operating at national level like Industrial Development Bank of India (IDBI), Industrial Financial Corporation of India (IFCI), Industrial Credit and Investment Corporation of India (ICIC1), Small Industrial Development Bank of India (SIDBI), and Industrial Investment Bank of India (IIBI).

THE GENESIS OF INDIAN DFIs

In India, the humble beginning of industrial DFI started with the establishment of IFCI in 1948 to give a shape to the shattered economy left by British's. It was the first DFI after Independence. It was established because normal banking accommodation was inappropriate and the recourse to capital issue methods was impracticable. It was conceived as a public institution controlled by the Government of India. After IFCI, ICICI came into existence in 1955 as a private sector DFI with the help of World Bank. ICICI was created to channeling the foreign currency loan to the Indian industries. In 1964, IDBI was established as a wholly owned Government enterprise to function as the apex financial institution in the capital market so far as term lending to industries is concerned. It was established to supplement the activities of the existing development banks and also to provide dynamic leadership in the task of promoting a widely dispersed and diversified and yet viable process of industrialisation (Bhatt, 1974). After IDBI, IRBI came into existence in 1985 to look after the rehabilitation of sick and closed industries. But with the functioning of BIFR i.e. Board for Industrial Financial Reconstruction, it became a full-fledged term lending institution at par with other institutions in 1997 and renamed as (IIBI). The latest addition to this was SIDBI in 1990, came into being as a wholly owned subsidiary of IDBI, to look after small scale industries. Besides, these national level DFIs, many DFIs like State Financial Corporations (SFCs), State Industrial Development Corporations (SIDCs) etc. came into existence in sixties and seventies.

THE ROLE AND FUNCTIONS OF DEVELOPMENT BANKS

As discussed in various literature development banks are the institutions to promote and finance enterprise in the private sector (Diamond, 1957). These are institutions, public or private, which have one of their principal functions, as the making of medium and long-term investment in the industrial projects (Boskey, 1959). These are financial intermediaries supplying finance to economic development of projects and providing related service (Kane, 1975). Development banks have two functions to perform i.e., banking and development. As banker the development banks are expected to finance those projects which are "Bankable" (Hook, 1976). A development bank must be an organic body that acts its appropriate place in the economy and create a proper image for itself with government, industry, agriculture and other sectors that serves.... The most important function of a development bank is to assist the process of development and the criterion of success is the extent to which it helps the process of the development of resources: human, material, regional and financial (Demissie, 1985).

These above observations revealed the pervasiveness of the nature of a development bank. The range of service varies from provision of medium and long-term loans to project appraisal and managerial and promotional assistance. However, despite their diverse nature, they have been devised to provide, at least a few if not all the fundamental ingredients of economic development, the lack or inadequacy of which may be inhibiting an accelerated pace of progress. Thus, a development bank is intended to provide the necessary capital, enterprise, managerial and technical know-how where these are inadequate or non-available and also assist in building up the financial and socio-economic infrastructure, favourable to quick economic development (Basu, 1965).

CHALLENGES POSED TO INDIAN DFIs

In the present transitional phase Indian DFIs have changed their perception of business. DFIs are now driven by commercial objectives and market forces. The role of a development financier has been modified to a great extent in response to new challenges. Besides India there are other examples, such as the Development Bank of Singapore (DBS), the Korea Long Term Credit Bank (KCB), the Industrial Financial Corporation of Thailand (IFCT), and the China Development Corporation (CDC) (Diamond, 1989).

The various areas where DFIs have found new challenges are:

Resource Mobilisation

One of the challenging aspects of Indian DFIs is resource mobilisation. Their success and failure depend on the ability to cope up with the growing needs of the industry and the overall economy and as a corollary to this it is necessary on the part of DFIs to have adequate resources. Raising resources at a cheaper rate has become a cause of concern for them. Particularly, after the phasing out of Govt. guaranteed bonds (SLR Bonds) and drying up of low-cost Long-Term Operation (LTO) funds from RBI, DFIs are raising funds at market related rates. In this way, DFIs have been forced to go both domestic and international markets. They have also started raising short-term loans subject to certain conditions. Amidst these changes the average cost of fund has become more which ultimately affected the net margin (Table 1). The low rate of margin reveals the complexity of the environment and really these years have been a crunch time for DFIs. However,

DFIs have managed to live in this type of situation. During the later part of nineties many of them have issued rupee bonds to Indian public like Deep Discount Bonds and Flexi Bonds by IDBI, Family Bonds by 1FCI etc. IDBI and ICICI have also made forays into foreign market with issue of Floating Rate Notes (FRNs) in European markets and Global Deposit Receipts (GDR) issues by ICICI. Recently, ICICI has listed in NYSE with an American Depository Receipt (ADR) of $100 million as the first Indian DFI. The mobilisation of resources at market related rates forced DFIs to innovate new products/services and to shift from developmental objective to commercial objective.

Product Diversification

The nineties have envisaged the keenness among the DFIs to provide wide range of products and services to the clients. New products have become more fee-based than fund based. The existing fund based products have been basically channeled to infrastructure and sunrise industries with high growth potential like pharmaceuticals, information technology, food processing etc. However, the focus has been more on non-project finance like equipment leasing, bridge loan, short-term loans, underwriting, guarantees, direct subscription to equity and debentures, corporate loans, asset credit, venture capital finance etc. Table-2 reveals the shift of activities in the DFIs. Till the end of 31-03-1990 the share of project loan was 48 per cent but during the last five years it has grown to around 55 per cent on an average. Similarly, the underwriting and direct subscription has made a quantum jump from 1.8 per cent to an average of 10 per cent during the same period. On an average 5 per cent of total disbursement made through short-term and bridge loan which was nil till 1990. Among the fee-based services merchant banking, debenture trusteeship, forex services, financial restructuring, mergers and acquisitions, project counseling, credit rating, retail banking etc. These activities are either carried on directly by DFIs themselves or by their subsidiaries (Chart-1). The IDBI and ICICI have also entered into new areas of business like commercial banking. Both of them have also tied with international insurance companies for insurance business in India. In 1996 ICICI even went one step ahead by establishing I- CREDIT, a non-banking finance company to create wide retail network to enter new areas like financing of automobiles, consumer durable, vendor lending and factoring services (IDBI, 1998-99). Thus it is found that the product portfolio has been restructured by DFIs for focused attention so that the deployment of scarce resources will properly fit to the market demand.

Shift in Basic Objectives

One of the important features of a development bank relates to the purpose for which funds are made available by it. The accent of these banks is on development so that its purpose is the provision of 'development finance', that is finance for new real investment on fixed assets (Om Prakash, 1957). By following an appropriate location policy, while assisting projects, they could help in reducing regional imbalance. In the initial years it was found that DFIs in India were disbursing almost 50 per cent of their assistance to backward areas. Till 1990 as shown in Table-2 the share of backward area was above 40 per cent. But during the recent years it has been gradually declining and reached merely at 26 per cent in 1996-97. It has also been found that a substantial portion of the assistance to the backward regions continues to flow to a small number of backward regions located conveniently nearer to the metropolitan or urban centers and having reasonably good infrastructure facilities and communications (Dave, 1983). Thus it seems that DFIs, are only interested in commercially attractive investments. It is also a fact that after the recommendation of the first

Narsimham Committee Report in 1992 to close the refinancing window, IDBI had made an attempt to do that. But the protest from SFCs and SIDCs halted that move. It is also a fact IDBI is saddled with refinance and lending commitments of thousand crore of rupees to SFCs which do not yield competitive returns. Table-2 reveals that till 1990 refinance was more than 38 per cent in total disbursement, which has gradually fallen down to around 8 per cent in 1998-99.

Prudential Norms

A major element of the financial sector reform in India has been the application of prudential norms and regulations introduced in 1992 aimed at ensuring safety and soundness of the financial system and at the same time encouraging markets to play increasing role. Prudential norms serve two primary purposes—first they reveal the true position of the bank's loan portfolio and secondly, they help arrest its deterioration. These norms introduced in India relate to income recognition, asset classification and provisioning for bad and doubtful debts and capital adequacy (RBI, 1997-98). Since 1993 Indian banks are required to adopt Basle Committee norms on capital adequacy by maintaining 8 per cent capital on the risk-weighted assets. But as per the acceptance of RBI, on the basis of the recommendation of Narasimham Committee Report II, now they have to maintain 9 per cent capital adequacy ratio by March 2000. Table-3 depicts the CAR of DFIs, which shows a declining, trend in last 3 years. This indicates that DFIs have to infuse more capital in future to maintain a comfortable ratio.

The quality of asset is also an important factor, which can not be ignored. The menace of non-performing assets, which reflects the asset quality, is a worldwide phenomenon. NPAs are nothing but the reflection of the economy and its performance. If the economy performs well, NPAs will be less whereas NPAs tend to rise in a recesionary environment. Table-3 reveals a high per centage of assets are in the category of NPAs i.e. substandard, doubtful and loss assets. Among the DFIs, SIDBI has the lowest NPAS, whereas others have more than 10 per cent. Since any NPA is bad, such a high per centage is definitely alarming for DFIs. A high quality of credit management skill is necessary prerequisite for protecting DFIs' assets from contamination. To tackle the growth of NPAs a comprehensive package of measure is required of all parties involved- DFI management, governments and central banks, as well as DFI creditors, which in most cases are multilateral development banks (Golan, 1988). At the individual level there is need of establishing a separate cell to exclusively handle the problem of distressed borrowers and to set up portfolio management system. Thus DFIs should make adequate provisions for dad and doubtful debts, as well as reflect realistic income flows by not accruing interest on such debts. This would provide a cleaner picture of their capital structure and cash flows (IDBI, 1996-97).

Spawning new institutions in Capital Market

The role of DFIs in nurturing Indian capital market through underwriting, direct subscription etc. needs no elaboration. They are also helping the new assisted units through these activities. As shown in Table-2, till 1990 the share of under writing and direct subscription was only 1.8 per cent in total disbursements of DFIs. But in recent years it has increased to 12.2 per cent, which indicates the growing participation by DFIs in capital market. The DFIs also initially undertake and subscribe to the equity capital became the suppliers of industrial securities to the market which include both personal investors and saving institutions. This development helped greatly to develop the secondary market by augmenting greatly the volume of trading on the stock exchange (Parekh, 1984). Simultaneously DFIs in India are also actively participating in sponsoring new institutions in capital market. In 1992 Securities and Exchange Board of India (SEBI) was established with active participation of DFIs to monitor the capital market activities and provide safeguard to investors. Similarly, in 1993 National Stock Exchange (NSE) was established for upliftment of debt/equity market through nation-wide screen based trading system. The much needed National Depository Limited was also came up in 1996 which usher an era of scripless on-line screen based trading with the help of IDBI and others.

Universal banking

In the post-financial sector reform era the DFIs in India have been gradually reorienting their focus from mere development banks to universal banks. The deregulation of interest rates, disintermediation and increasing participation by commercial banks in project finance has significantly altered the traditional operating environment for DFIs. Recently, they have entered into the realm of working capital or short term financing by breaking the "great divide" between commercial banks and DFIs. After the drying up of govt-guaranteed bonds and LTO funds from RBI, DFIs have targeted the same segment of commercial banks i.e. household sector. They are vying for lifting the ceiling on raising short-term funds from the market and remove the restrictions so as to bring them par with commercial banks. On the other side commercial banks are demanding statutory reserve requirements on DFIs in relation to short-term funds. This indicates that gradually the gap between them is narrowing down in both the fields of resource mobilisation and resource deployment. The Second Narasimham Report, 1998 and S.H. Khan, Working Group on harmonising the roles of banks and financial institutions, 1998 have recommended for convergence of activities between DFIS and Banks over a period of time which will be a gradual move towards universal banking (RBI, 1998).

VISION FOR TOMORROW

It is envisaged from the fact that Indian economy will continue to grow at a faster pace because the economy has shown resilience during the political instability phase. The growth will much faster when second phase of reform take a concrete shape. In the coming years it is thus expected that financial sector vis-a-vis the DFIs will undergo greater metamorphosis. The emphasis on commercialisation of activities will further dominate the developmental objectives of these DFIs. Developments like leasing of own assets, factoring of loan, merger and acquisitions among DFIs and commercial banks, issue of commercial papers, collaborations with commercial banks, loans to borrowers with profit sharing features etc. will take place. And most likely the information technology will dominate the operational activities. Networking of some of the key branches would be a vital area of importance. And in this process of transformation clearly the fast-movers will be always in the advantageous position. Among the DFIs in India ICICI is rising at faster rate than others. Perhaps the advantage of being in private sector helping it in quick decision making and to venture into new business.

REFERENCES

1. Bhatt, V. V., "A Decade Performance of IDBI", *Commerce,* Annual Number, 1974, p.151.
2. Diamond, William., *Development Banks,* Baltimore, John Hopkins Press, 1974, pp.4-5.
3. Boskey, Shirly., *Problems and Practices of Development Banks,* Baltimore, John Hopkins Press, 1959, p. 9.
4. Kane, Joseph. A., *Development Banking,* Laxington Books, D.C. Heath and Company, 1975, pp. 14-15.

5. Hook, J.T.D., *Financing and Problems of Development Banking,* New York, F. A. Prager Publisher, 1976, p.2.
6. Demissie, Asfa. "The Role, Function and Purpose of Development Banks", The *International Journal of Development Banking* (IJDB), ICICI, Bombay, Vol.3, January 1985, pp.43-44.
7. Basu, S.K., *Theory and Practice of Development Banking,* Bombay, Asia Publishing House, 1965, p. 1.
8. Diamond, William, "Agenda for Development Financing in the 1990s", ADFIAP *Journal of Development Finance,* Asia-Pacific, December-89. pp.11-18.
9. Om Prakash, "Industrial Development Corporations in India and Pakistan", *Economic Journal,* Vol.1, No. xviii, 1957, p.40.
10. Dave, S. A., "Challenges of Development Banking", S.K. Monoranjan Memorial Lecture Delivered in Sydenham College of Commerce and Economics, 15-12-1983, Bombay.
11. IDBI, *Report on Development Banking,* 1996-97.
12. RBI, *Report on Trend and Progress of Banking in India,* 1997-98, p. 32.
13. Golan, Amon, "The World Bank Perspective", *ADFIAP Journal of Development Finance,* Special Issue, October 1988, p.9.
14. Parekh, H.T., "Development Finance: Retrospect and Prospect", *IJDB,* Vol.2, No.1, January 1984, pp.35.
15. RBI, *Supplement to RBI Bulletin,* November 1998, p.29.

Table 1

Average Cost of Fund

(In%)

Year/DFIs	*IDBI*	*IFCI*	*ICICI*	*SIDBI*	*IIBI*
1994-95	8.1	9.5	9.1	10.0	10.0
	3.2	*6.2*	*4.2*	*3.9*	*2.1*
1995-96	8.4	10.8	9.2	10.2	8.8
	3.7	*6.9*	*3.9*	*3.9*	*1.0*
1996-97	8.9	12.9	9.5	10.4	10.5
	3.7	*5.7*	*4.0*	*4.2*	*3.7*
1997-98	8.7	11.5	9.8	10.2	10.6
	3.9	*4.4*	*4.2*	*4.2*	*4.8*
1998-99	9.0	11.7	10.1	10.5	10.3
	2.6	*2.4*	*3.9*	*3.5*	*3.6*

Note: Figures in italic indicate net margin of DFIs.

Source: IDBI, Report on development banking in India, 1998-99.

Table 2

Share in total disbursement of DFIs

In%

Year/Item	*Project Loan**	*U'writing & D. Sub*	*Bridge/ST Loan*	*Backward Area Fin'g*	*Refinancing*
1992-93	52.3	2.6	10.3	34.1	13.5
1993-94	46.6	4.7	15.1	30.0	12.4
1994-95	41.5	11.3	23.3	31.9	8.5
1995-96	59.7	10.0	4.5	32.3	9.9
1996-97	55.0	5.9	1.8	26.0	6.8
1997-98	60.6	13.7	8.2	NA	7.1
1998-99	60.9	12.2	5.3	NA	7.6
Till 1990	48.0	1.8	-	43.7	38.6

*Project loan includes Direct Rupee Loan and Foreign Currency Loan.

Source: IDBI Report on Development Banking in 1989-90, 1994-95, and 1998-99.

Table 3

Capital Adequacy Ratio & Non Performing Asset of DFIs*

In%

DFI	*IDBI*		*IFCI*		*ICICI*		*SIDBI*		*IIBI*	
YEAR	*CAR*	*NPA*	*CAR*	*NPA*	*CAR*	*NPA*	*CAR*	*NPA*	*CAR*	*NPA*
1994-95	12.4	7.8	14.4	10.0	109	6.9	14.0	-	21.8	-
1995-96	15.9	9.4	12.4	NA	10.1	11.7	21.0	2.8	15.9	NA
1996-97	14.7	10.3	10.1	NA	13.2	7.8	25.7	4.6	10.6	NA
1997-98	13.7	10.1	11.6	13.6	13.0	7.7	25.7	4.1	12.8	13.0
1998-99	12.7	12.0	8.4	21.0	12.5	7.8	26.9	3.5	11.7	14.0

*Assets which are not standard.

Source: IDBI Report on Development Banking in India, 1998-99.

CHART-1

IDBI

* Credit Analysis and Research Ltd.
* Investor Service of India Ltd.
* IDBI Investment Management Company India Ltd.
* IDBI Capital Market Service Ltd.
* IDBI Bank Ltd.
* IDBI Intech Ltd.

IFCI

* Investment Information and Credit Rating Agency of India Ltd.
* IFCI Financial Services Ltd.
* IFCI Custodial Services Ltd.
* IFCI Investor Services Ltd.

ICICI

* Credit Rating and Information Services Ltd.
* ICICI Credit Corporation Ltd.

* ICICI Trust Ltd.
* ICICI Banking Corporation Ltd.
* ICICI Asset Management Company Ltd.
* ICICI Infotech.
* ICICI Securities and Finance Company Ltd.
* ICICI Web Trading.
* ICICI Investor Services Ltd.

9

MARKETING IN BANKS — THE CHALLENGES AHEAD

—MS. APARA SHARMA & R.K.GUPTA

Banking has come a long way from brick and mortar structure to sophisticated automated teller machines, internet banking and touch screen kiosks facilitating transactions. With the evergrowing new avenues of investment, offering the ease of withdrawal of funds before maturity, safety and attractive returns, banks are facing tough times. Mutual funds, and equity share market are posing serious threats to the Fixed Deposit schemes of banks. Customer has become aware of these new avenues and is also ready to diversify his portfolio. He has also come along way from his grandfather who deposited money in a post office scheme or a fixed deposit and felt satisfied that his money was safe and also bearing adequate returns. Now the whole scenario has changed. Even the attitude of customers has witnessed a sea change. Marketing of bank services is not a new phenomenon but it has certainly assumed new dimensions.

Marketing broadly refers to a way of managing a business so that each strategy or service is evolved with fore knowledge of the impact that the decision has upon customers. It is all about persuading people to avail the services that an organization is offering. A service in

Kotler's words can be defined, as thus, "A service is any activity or benefit that one party can offer to another that is essentially intangible and does not result in the ownership of anything." They are intangible, inseparable, heterogeneous and perishable. Viewed in this light, it is very important area in relation to banking since the crux of retail banking in today's scenario is marketing.

The hindrances to marketing in Indian scenario involved regulatory approach of the Reserve Bank of India, dominance of social banking, conservative approach and absence of innovative banking. However, India could not remain untouched by the changes all over the globe. With liberalisation in 1991 having ushered in, the conventional inward looking banking system took a backstage. In this paper, we attempt to study the issues involved in marketing in retail banking for a customer and a banker.

Broadly marketing in retail banking involves

* Explaining the services offered through oral and written methods
* Offering the benefits available in addition to the main services
* Clarifying the bank charges involved
* Explaining the stipulations involved
* Selling the service at a competitive price
* Retaining the customer

Therefore, it can broadly be divided into 'what' and 'how' of marketing with focus on banking services. The 'what' part deals with the peculiar features of retail products of banking as compared with consumer durables and the 'how' part deals with the actual interface. The 'how' part logically draws from the 'what' part and therefore has to be dealt first.

Indian financial market is in a transitional phase. In such times, Retail Banking has assumed new dimensions. Marketing of bank services needs to be focused at if banks are to retain customer and also keep their profitability ratios attractive to the shareholders.

Marketing is basically helping people to buy and not 'telling them to buy.' For example, if a customer walks into a departmental store, he is not to be convinced to buy, rather to be assisted in choosing from the various products available.

Similarly, when a customer walks into a bank, the products have to be marketed persuasively.

There are some crucial issues, which need attention when talking about banking services.

* First of all, there is not much flexibility that can be allowed to the customer when it comes to basic guidelines that are to be followed by a customer. For example, as per the guideline issued by the Reserve Bank of India (effective October 1, 2001), a bank cannot pay interest on the maturity amount of a fixed deposit in case one month lapses and the customer does not get it renewed. Hence he stands to lose if he does not instruct his bank to renew his fixed deposit within one month of the date of maturity. Now, this is a very typical case where customer needs to be explained and convinced. No amount of flexibility can be allowed as far as such regulations are concerned with relation to banking.
* Another issue involved in marketing of baking services is that being a service industry, how products are marketed. This involved the skills of the front officers who have to market effectively.
* Third, unlike and exquisite jewellery showroom where only the upper middle class or upper class clients are expected to pay a visit, a banker can

expect a whole range of customer ranging from a watchman who has opened a recurring deposit of one thousand rupees who approaches the bank for premature withdrawal to a Non Resident Indian who urgently wants his remittance from USA. Now dealing with these two clients at the same time has to be done tactfully and effectively.

* Finally, a major issue involved in banking service is that they are dealing with public money. They not only allow transactions but also act as custodians of saving of the public. And therefore are accountable not only to the public but also to the Government of the country.

Considering all these issues, one can relate to marketing of bank services as a differentiated activity. One needs to focus on the 'how' part as well as the content of marketing of such services. Patrick Forsyth in his book '*Communicating with Customers*' aptly remarks that out of one hundred dissatisfied customers, only five complain while ninety five never come back. Now, these ninety-five customers are equally important. One needs to look at the needs of these customers since these are the one 'who will never come back.' They will not create a scene but would rather deal with some other bank. As such banking being a service industry, marketing has to be done not only at the point of sale but also the follow up part. It is equally important or rather more crucial to retain customers. This leads to long-term relations where lies the crux of banking.

Banks are offering a wide range of produces. These vary from liquid fixed deposits, debit cards, internet banking to single window investment portfolio. The era of Relationship Banking is here to day where a high net worth client is handled by and exclusive manager who assists him in selecting the optimum portfolio. Banks are also entering the field of mobile banking where bills can be deposited online. E-commerce, mobile banking, telephone banking are internet banking restrict the number of visits that a customer makes to the bank. Therefore, when he walks into the premises to avail a specific service like getting a demand draft made, he definitely needs attention.

An important factor in marketing is 'promise less than you can deliver' and then 'deliver more than you have promised.' This, if seen in the context of the customer who has just walked in can be illustrated as thus. In first case, when he approaches a front desk executive, the latter being an aggressive salesman asks him to have a seat where he will get the demand draft within five minutes. The customer is short of time and feels good that his work will be done immediately. However, fifteen minutes pass and he still does not get the demand draft. He feels agitated and approaches the front officer. The latter apologizes profusely and hands over the demand draft after a lapse of another five minutes. The customer walks out and the image of the bank is certainly tarnished. In a second case, the same customer walks in, the front officer asks him to wait and clearly but politely informs that it would take ten minutes. The customer takes a seat and the demand draft is handed over to him within eight minute. He feels very good and decides to open another saving account with his wife in the same branch of the bank. Therefore, the conclusion to be drawn is that customer has to be treated as a logical entity. He has to be informed about the exact situation. He does not mind waiting if he has been informed beforehand.

An officer in a bank always has to remember that he is the representative of the bank. Any vague statement can tarnish the image of the bank. In this context, phone ethics can also not be ignored.

Another dimension in bank services is the print media. With so many financial institutions diversifying into retail banking, marketing has never been so challenging. Apart from facing the challenges from other range of financial services, banks face competition amongst themselves. However, this would require another set of discussions and a different angle.

While dealing with customers, a banker needs to be well informed about the customers apart from his own information about bank services. He ought to be concerned and interested. He needs to offer alternatives. He needs to be open to the demands of the customers. He has to inform the customer regarding any bank charges or hidden costs to avoid any confusion in later stages.

Training can also be resorted to in the competitive era of banking. Human resource is a dynamic resource, which needs to be harnessed effectively. With the era of information technology having dawned on the Indian shores, one is sure of the automation of banks within a certain time frame. However, the edge now lies in managing human resource that will in turn market the products of the banks to the public in general.

With special reference to Indian scenario where market is fragmented and diverse. The market segmentation is crucial for Indian scenario. An important aspect in favour of banks in India is that the traditional investor poses all his trust in the Fixed Deposit Receipts issued to customers. With the volatility in financial markets, the depression in the market in general and uncertainty of returns from various investments, a bank can certainly turn the situation by effectively marketing the services. Banks approach towards customers has undergone a change in focus. They have shifted to marketing their services and have adopted a market-oriented approach. Banks should professionally shape and adequate structure for marketing in banking where reaching out to customers and creating awareness about the various services available is focused at.

Banks need to reorganize themselves structurally and attitudewise if they aim to survive in this competitive environment.

The need of the hour is to jump headlong into the market fully equipped with various tacts of marketing including price, promotion, place and product. The general principles of marketing certainly apply to marketing of bank services but as specified earlier, they need to be applied in a different manner. The relation of Banker and Customer is not a one-time transaction but a lifelong relation where the customer reposes his confidence in the bank as trustee of his funds. Such relation can be ensured if marketing of bank services is seen and treated as an ongoing process of converting walk-in clients to lifelong valued customers.

10

MARKETING STRATEGY FOR INDIAN RURAL BANKING

—R.D. SHARMA & MS. RASHMI SHARMA

Marketing Strategy for Indian rural banking is a composite of banking services, widely known as marketing mix, suitable to people of rural India and also capable of meeting institutional objectives in the light of fast changes in the requirements of rural bank customers of different socio-economic profile. Such a marketing strategy needs to be regularly monitored and reviewed to keep the rural banks effective and viable.

In fact Government of India started rural banking services on massive scale in 1975 by launching low cost Regional Rural Banks (RRBs) on the recommendations by a working group when the efforts of commercial and cooperative banks failed to meet the growing needs of the planned economy, particularly, the needs of the target groups. At present 196 RRBs are operating in the country by covering 427 districts through a huge network of 14,581 branches. After a long history of about more than two decades of chronic sickness, these banks have started showing some improvement. In terms of deposit mobilisation and extension of loans, 188 of these banks showed better performance. Though the amount of total losses of all the RRBs came down from Rs. 3047 crores in 1997 to Rs. 310 crores as on March 31, 1998 yet, there is lot of scope for still better improvement if a marketing strategy of suitable marketing mix and efforts for creating a sound work culture, duly supported with a disciplined skilled and motivated manpower, well trained employees for delivering specialised services in rural setting, coordinated operations in bank branches, strong marketing organisation as per the requirements of rural banks, information about customers expectations, creative selling and cost effective system (Bhattacharya 1989; Bhatt 1991; Mandanna 1993) is designed so that the problems of negative spread or margin, inadequate business mechanism etc. can be checked. In this regard Government of India (GOI) and RBI have initiated several schemes of rural banking services in the light of recommendations of various committees for all round and integrated development of rural sector through RRBs but the given mechanism of rural banking structure does not serve the rural masses effectively in terms of marketing concept of rural banking in Indian perspective (Sharma, Desh Bandhu and Kaur 1999). It is in this context that the present study for working out marketing strategy for Indian rural banking needs to be carried on for socio-economic development of rural India.

REVIEW OF LITERATURE

Sharma *et al.* (1998), in their study based on primary information gathered through Five Point Likert Scale (5←----→1) from 600 randomly selected respondents from a village of Jammu District suggest three tier strategy for designing, delivering and monitoring rural bank services to enable the RRBs to achieve institutional objectives with customer satisfaction. However, paper does not cover the marketing practices of cooperative and commercial banks operating in rural India.

According to Parasuraman (2000), today the customers have to serve themselves through technological based system, but this does not mean that companies can afford to ignore service. On the contrary, the growth of self-service technologies calls for a heightened emphasis on customer service. This paper gave clue regarding better service quality but does not tell in what proportion marketing mix elements i.e. price, product, place and promotion are to be combined in order to form well designed marketing strategy.

Smithamy *et. al.* (1999) suggested as to how customer can be satisfied again in case of service failure but does not facilitate strategy for marketing efforts in rural banking services.

Kaur (1999) determined the nature and extent of marketing orientation with reference to the whole of the package of rural banking services and suggested strategic action plan for overall culture of marketing in these banks. However it has not covered all the types of rural banks. Moreover, basic objective of suggesting a marketing strategy for overall effective functioning vis-a-vis customer satisfaction has not been adequately a ddressed.

Jain and Sharma (2000) highlighted that product related antecedents and sources of consumer involvement are very important for making marketing decisions and formulating strategies. However, the study is related to only three products preferred by the upper class people having relatively higher level of education. This paper has direct relevance to proposed topic of research particularly the antecedents of consumer involvement in rural banking services. The methodology of the said paper has been duly considered in the proposed research.

Zeithaml *et al.* (1996) examined the effect of service quality on behavioural consequences, with the objective to find out the evidence regarding impact of behavioural consequences of service quality on the customer. The paper provides useful information regarding the quality of service to be provided to the customers so that they continue to remain with the banks.

Parasuraman *et al.* (1985) suggested a model which would help the marketers in measuring service quality. In the light of various dimensions identified by A. Parasuraman, Valarie A Zeithaml & Leonard L. Berry, the marketing strategy would be worked out with reference to rural banking.

Norburn David *et al.* (1988) highlighted that irrespective of national origin companies that are close to their customers, have similar corporate values and focus on external marketing are those that demonstrate superior strategy of marketing effectiveness. The conclusions drawn might have been different if developing countries would have been covered. The study has relevance to the topic of research and its objective with regard to marketing strategy of rural banking in context to customer closeness and external marketing etc.

JUSTIFICATION

The marketing strategy for Indian rural banking has to be formulated on the basis of first hand information from the actual beneficiaries of these banks and published/unpublished information from their annual reports and publications of RBI will prove to be useful to the bankers, policy makers and for future research. Such a study is expected to provide badly needed guidelines for the better functioning of these banks by identifying their present weak areas within the domain of rural bank marketing. Similarly the research design supported with needed reliability and validity measures will prove to be useful addition to the existing knowledge of rural bank marketing necessary for bankers to ensure effective banking services in rural India.

OBJECTIVES

The study has been undertaken primarily with the objective of formulating marketing strategy for banking services in rural India as in spite of several remedies initiated by GOI including infusion of capital to RRBs as per recommendations of various committees, their performance remains dismal. (Reddy *et al.* 1998) due to lack of planned marketing efforts (Sharma 1995). The various objectives within this broader objective of the study appear to be as under:

1. Rural banks have not been able to enjoy a reasonable level of banking business (Reddy *et al.* 1998). Hence first objective is:

   To work out marketing strategy for increasing the market potential for rural banking services,

2. Although the recommendations of various committee have been implemented for improving the overall functioning of rural banks, but their impact in the form of socio-economic development in their areas of operation is not much encouraging (Kaur 1999). Thus, next objective:

   To identify the causes of failures and accordingly chalk out a strategy for all round development of rural masses through loanable bank schemes.

3. The promotional activities of Rural banks for creating awareness among the rural masses and building confidence among them about credibility and effectiveness in the operations of these banks have not yet received adequate attention of the people (Sharma *et al.* 1999). Hence next objective:

   To work out a suitable promotional strategy so that rural masses feel encouraged in availing of rural bank services.

4. Besides rural banks the cooperative banks operating in rural areas have suffered heavily due to lack of

professionalised skill and operational efficiency (Patel, 2001). Therefore next objective:

To identify various aspects of banking operations viz., deposit mobilisation and lending operation etc. wherein needed personnel training requirements are determined by the respective rural/cooperative banks.

5. Roa *et al.* (2000) observed overall inefficiency in rural banks due to lack of customer orientation among bank personnel. Hence, next objective:

   To work out customer orientation strategy at different levels of rural banking system.

6. Although rural banks have shown better performance in terms of deposit mobilisation and extension of loans during recent years, yet amount of losses of all the RRBs in the country has not been completely controlled. It was estimated as high as Rs. 310 crores on March 31, 1998 (Bhattacharya *et al.* 1989). Therefore, next objective:-

   To identify most viable projects in rural areas against which bank loans should be sanctioned.

7. There is close relationship between the socio-economic profile of the customers and their behaviour towards different products/services they buy (Jain *et al.* 2000). Thus, there is a need:

   To identify various socio-ecomomic factors affecting the selection of different rural banking services by rural people.

HYPOTHESES

The existing literature indicates the main hypothesis of study that Indian rural banking lacks effectiveness due to, among other factors, inadequate marketing culture in their workings (Sharma *et al.* 1999). The corollaries that flow from the main hypothesis:

1. As compared to other marketing efforts by Indian rural banks, their promotional activities have neither been given adequate attention nor effectively deployed wherever was possible (Sharma *et al.* 1999). Hence first hypothesis:

   Promotional efforts by Indian rural banks have not been ever planned in light of their relevance to rural market.

2. The procedural formalities in opening bank accounts and for obtaining financial support from rural banks have been uncomfortable and time consuming (Roa, *et al.* 2000). Hence:

   Procedural formalities in rural banks have discouraged the rural masses for availing of banking services.

3. The rural bank employees have not been properly trained to serve the rural masses as per their socio-economic conditions (Patel 2001). Hence:

   Bank personnel operating in rural areas lack professional skill and knowledge in serving their clients.

4. At present 196 RRBs are operating through about 15000 branches only in 427 districts in the country indicating thereby sufficient scope of more branches in rural areas (Reddy *et al.* 1998). Hence:

   There is sufficient uncovered rural market for Indian consumer banks.

5. Since rural masses are spread over a large area along with vast social, economic, cultural and agro-ecological diversities, no straight jacket blue print of any uniform banking model can prove to be efficient to meet area- specific needs (Patel 2001). Hence next hypothesis:

The bank branches operating in rural India have succeeded quite marginally in meeting area— specific requirements of the people belonging to different socio-cultural and agro-ecological profile.

6. Rural banks are facing problem of mounting over dues. Because out of the 49 RRBs selected for revamping under phase one the profits of 5 RRBs declined during 1994-95 compared to 1993-94, while 18 banks had increased their losses during 1994-95 and 1993-94 sharing deterioration in the performance of 23 banks (Reddy *et al.* 1998). Hence:

   The rural banks have not yet identified the major causes of mounting overdues so that a remedial measure could be worked out.

7. Many intervening factors including non-professionalised attitude of bank personnel and lack of relationship-marketing efforts have affected adversely the customers satisfaction and their loyalty with these banks. Hence:

   Absence of professionalised skill and lack of relationship marketing efforts lead to lower customer satisfaction and lack of loyalty.

PLAN OF THE STUDY

The order to judiciously address the objectives and hypotheses formulated, this study can be organised in the following eight chapters:

The introductory chapter should present status of marketing strategy of Indian rural banking wherein till date efforts for designing, maintaining and delivering the socio-economically relevant banking services by different agencies at central and grass root levels will be examined in detail and finally the same will be summarised as the base for working out the needed changes for future.

The relevant literature on marketing strategy in services with special reference to consumer banking need to be reviewed in the second chapter for tracing the research gap both in terms of methodology and dimensions of strategic marketing efforts. For these research papers from different journals like journal of marketing, Journal of consumer research etc. ought to be reviewed for the formulation of research objectives and hypotheses.

The various aspects of research design and methodology, viz., nature of information required for the study of explanation about the research population and sample size, selection of respondents, construction of data collection form, various statistical tools including procedure of data purification and finalisation of scale, reliability and validity of research etc. should be presented in third chapter of the thesis.

The fourth chapter on consumer banking products need to consolidate the present level of product adequacy and suitability in terms of customer judgement and experience and accordingly it should facilitate the formulation of a strategy for need based banking services in rural India (Sharma *et al.* 1999).

The various issues concerning the determination of bank deposit rates, interest on loans, commission charges, collection charges etc. ought to be addressed in fifth chapter within the framework of customer orientation in the context of rural bank marketing efforts. This chapter should also provide a strategy for making this price mix decisions more competitive, attractive and responsive to rural settings (Patel 2001).

As per Indian rural banking policy the rural bank branches are being established at the doorsteps of rural masses as per local requirements for banking services particularly for the financial support to them for establishing income and employment generating units. Therefore chapter sixth need to be devoted to the measurement of marketing efforts for effective services delivery through these branches in terms of bank personnel attitude, facilities in the branches, layout, fixture and other aspects of branch interior and exterior.

Promotion mix element has not received much attention of policy makers and administrators of rural bank as compared to other marketing mix elements. So seventh chapter ought to be devoted to marketing strategy for promotion mix containing details about various promotional tools to be employed in Indian rural banking services.

The eighth chapter should measure the responsiveness of the bank personnel to the rural banking needs, their friendly attitude towards customers and competence, operational effectiveness etc. within the framework of social concept of rural banking and finally a strategy need to be formulated in this chapter to make the bank personnel close to the rural markets in terms of language, beliefs and attitudes (Patel, 2001).

The various aspects of banking procedures and formalities like loan documents, time taken in completing these formalities, cost involved etc. ought to be examined within the domain of effectiveness of marketing efforts in ninth chapter. The strategic action plan to make various process mix issues customer friendly and comfortable should be presented in this chapter (Kotler, 1994).

NATURE AND SOURCES OF INFORMATION

The data for the study on the formulation of marketing strategy for Indian rural banks has to be gathered from both primary and secondary sources. The information regarding the nature and quality of marketing efforts in these banks should be collected through two different sets of schedule from bank customers and the bankers. Similarly the information regarding current position of the banks in terms of deposits mobilised, loans disbursed, branch network, profitability etc. should be obtained from banks annual reports, RBI publications like Basic Banking Statistics, Tables relating to Banks, Trends and Progress of Banking, RBI Bulletins, Selected Banking Indicators etc.

RESEARCH POPULATION, SAMPLE, SIZE AND SELECTION OF RESPONDENTS

The topic of research, as explained earlier, indicates two types of research population, viz., rural bank customers and the bank personnel working in the rural branches of Indian consumer banks (ICBs) as both of them are true and effective evaluators of the quality of marketing efforts made by these banks in their rural sector operations. In order to maintain exhaustiveness and objectivity in the study; a village level area can be selected for gathering information from about 10% of total households to be selected randomly. The village has got to be an ideal one in terms of presence of rural banking services from all the three types of ICBs. viz., commercial banks, regional rural banks, and cooperative banks. Similarly about 100 bank personnel working in rural branches of ICBs in the similar area may be contacted for information about the research problem in question.

GENERATION OF SCALE ITEMS

The various items covering all dimensions of marketing strategy in Indian rural banking have to be generated from the relevant literature and discussions with experts as per the research design and the two schedules to be administrated to the bank customers and the bankers. The various dimensions for the generation of these items include rural bank products, deposits and loan interest rates, other bank charges like commission and collection charges, effectiveness in various transactions, bank personnel behaviour, nature and effectiveness of communication with the target market etc., falling within the framework of latest model of marketing mix. More than 100 items should be generated so that factor analysis with reasonable and stable factor design could come up for the formulation of the strategy.

PURIFICATION OF SCALE ITEMS

For the formulation of an effective marketing strategy the information gathered through the aforesaid schedules should be subjected to factor analysis i.e. marketing mix element wise dimensionality of the various items of the scale on the overall as well component wise effectiveness of marketing strategy. The principal axis procedure of factor analysis needs to be used along with varixam rotation. After a series of several iterations as per factorial processing final meaningful and stable factors should be selected and the items with high loadings on more than one factor ought to be dropped. Thus, after recognizing the relative importance of each statement the factor loadings with less than 0.5 should be ignored.

VALIDITY AND RELIABILITY OF DATA

The convergent validity ought to be tested by analysing the degree of association between over-all effectiveness of marketing and variable-wise/marketing mix ingredient-wise effectiveness of marketing efforts in Indian rural banking. The relationship between dependent and independent variables has to be worked out with the help of coefficient of correlation and the strength of association with the help of coefficient of determination. The F-test has also to be used to determine the degree of equality of various dimensions in contributing over all marketing effectiveness. 't' test should be used to find out the significance of factors of six Ps in the formulation of marketing strategy.

LIMITATIONS

Though utmost care ought to be exercised at all the phases of research yet the following limitations need to be taken care of whenever the present study is referred to:

1. The study is area specific with regards to rural banking services i.e. its application in other areas of the countries has to be reviewed in the light of the sample and area profile.
2. The domain of marketing efforts has been determined on the basis of extended marketing mix comprising six Ps as per available literature but with the ongoing fast changes in rural banking services the present domain will prove to be incomplete.
3. Respondents may hesitate to give information regarding their dealings with the banks.
4. Managers of the banks may not provide correct information whenever their any performance in different banking services is not satisfactory.

REFERENCES

Bashier, Seema (1996). "*The Role of National Banks for Agriculture and Rural Development in Rural Sector- A Comparative Study of Jammu and Kashmir and Himachal Pradesh*, (Unpublished Ph.D thesis, University of Jammu), pp. 12-13.

Cundiff Edward W; Richard R. Still and Narman A.P Govoni (1980). *Fundamentals of Modern Marketing*. Prentice Hall of India. New Delhi, pp.358-373

Jain, K. Sanjay and Kavita Sharma (2000). "Product Related Antecedents of Consumer Involvement : An Empirical Investigation", Vikalpa, Vol.25, No. l, (Jan-March), pp. 29-41.

Kaur, Gurjeet (1999). "Marketing Orientation for Regional Rural Banks in Northern India—A Case Study of J&K and Punjab States", (Unpublished Ph.D Thesis, University of Jammu), pp. 1-364.

McCarthy, Edward (1971). *Basic Marketing and Managerial Approach*. Homewood, p. 6.

Norburn David, Sue Birley and Mark Dunn (1998), "Strategic Marketing Effectiveness and Its Relationship to Corporate Culture and Beliefs: A Cross National Study", *International Studies of Management and Organisation,* Vol. XVIII, pp. 30-97.

Parasuraman, A. (2000). "Superior Customer Service and Marketing Excellence: Two Sides of the Same Success Coin", *Vikalpa,* Vol. 25, No. 3, (July-Sept), pp. 3-13.

Patel, A.R. (2001). "Rural Credit System: Need For Restructing", *Kurukshetra,* Vol. 49, No. 4, (Jan), pp. 16-21.

Parasuraman, A, Valarie A. Zeithaml, Leonard L. Berry (1985). "A Conceptual Model of Service Quality and Its Implications for Future Research". *Journal of Marketing*. Vol. 49, pp. 41-50.

Roa, K. Dinker; R. Das Gupta; D.P. Khankhoje and N. B. Shete (2000). "Rural Economy in New Millennium and Challenges for Banks". *Prajnan,* Vol. XXVIII, No. 4.

Reddy, Ramachandra B; B.Sakunathala and S.Vijayulu Reedy (1998). "Growth and Performance of Regional Rural Banks in India". *Journal of Commerce,* Vol. 51, No. 293, (April-September), pp. 16-21.

Swith Amy K; Ruth N.,Balton and Janet Wagner (1999). *A Model of Customer Satisfaction with Service Encounters Involving Failure and Recovery,* Vol. XXXVI, (August), pp. 356-372.

Shainesh, G. and Mukul Mathur (2000). "Service Quality Measurement: The Case of Railway Freight Services", *Vikalpa,* Vol. 25, No. 3, (July-Sept), pp. 15-21.

Sharma, R.D. (1996). "Marketing Effectiveness in American Banks". *Prajnan,* Vol. XXIV, No. 2, pp. 149-156.

———,Desh Bandhu and Gurjeet Kaur (1998). "Marketing Orientation Strategy for Rural Banks: A Case Study", *Prajnan,* Vol. XXVII, No. 1, (April-June), pp. 47-99.

—,------ and ------ (1999). "Evaluation of Inbuilt Marketing Orientation in Indian Rural Marketing", *Abhigyan,* Vol. XVIII, No. 3, pp. 33-37.

Wadhva, Charan D(1980). *Rural Banks for Rural Development,* Macmillan, Madras, pp. 1-24.

Zeithaml Valarie A, Leonard L. Berry and A. Parasuraman (1996). "The Behavioural Consequences of Service Quality", *Journal of Marketing,* Vol. 60 (April), pp. 31-46.

11

IMPACT OF RELATIONSHIP MARKETING ON SATISFACTION AND LOYALTY IN URBAN INDIAN CONSUMER BANKING

—R.D. SHARMA & SHWETA GUPTA

In the highly globalised and liberalized economy, the customers are exposed to a flood of information unleashed on them from different sources, informing them about new products/services, new versions and uses of existing ones etc. (Ramaswamy and Namakumari ,1995). Such an information flow makes them 'well informed' and 'demanding' and thus difficult for the marketer to satisfy. These customers prefer suppliers who provide not just the core service but certain important peripherals too (Kotler 1999). Any apathetic attitude of the marketers towards the expectations of the clients would lead to dissatisfaction and consequently, receding customer loyalty. In such a competitive arena, the only key to continue enjoying customer patronage is maintaining long term, mutually beneficial relationship with the clients. Thus, the focus of marketing is shifting from 'creating exchanges' i.e., 'Transactional Marketing' to 'Relationship Marketing' (Panigrahy 2000). The conventional transactional marketing is a part of relationship marketing, which is a larger concept aiming at building long term mutually satisfying relations with key parties viz. customers, suppliers and distributors to earn and retain their long term preference (Kotler 1999). Relationship Marketing helps to attain a sustainable competitive advantage for the marketer (Morgan and Hunt 1999). It encourages a match between seller's competitive advantage and buyer's requirements over the life cycle of the item being purchased. Relationship Marketing develops reasons for the buyer to consider the service provider more than a source of single transaction, but rather as a dependable source for fulfilling many needs (Panigrahy 2000). Relationship marketing helps in building sound ties with the customers (Kotler 1999) and thus ensures that even if in a particular service encounter the service provider is not able to give his best, his customers will continue to patronize his services (Mishra 2000).

REVIEW OF LITERATURE

Crosby and Stephens (1987) in their study entitled "Effects of Relationship Marketing on Satisfaction, Retention and Prices in the Life Insurance Industry", have collected data through various stages viz., double postcards, questionnaires, telephone interviews and finally mail survey. The data is then analyzed by path analysis and structural equation analysis. The models suggested in the study are of much help to the proposed research due to the interactions and communications identified as effective in establishing strong relations with the customers.

"Developing Measures for Service Quality and Relationship Strength Determinants of Customer Loyalty" by Mookerjee and Shainesh (2000) identifies the determinants of relationship strength after collecting information separately on service quality, loyalty and relationship strength and then duly analyzing it through regression analysis using SPSS package. These determinants together with those identified in the proposed study will help in the formulation of Relationship Marketing strategy for banks.

The study entitled "Predictability and Personalization in the Service Encounter" by Suprenant and Solomon (1987) is based on the respondent's reactions to pre-recorded tapes presenting certain banking transactions. The three personalization strategies suggested in the paper can be of much use in the proposed study as personalization is an important part of relationship building. But the study is not exhaustive as all respondents belong to the same age group and educational background. Also, there is lack of direct involvement of the respondents due to simulated banking environment. Involving real service environment and selecting respondents from varied backgrounds will cover the gaps.

The paper "Relationship Quality and Buyer Seller Interactions in Channels of Distribution" by Jap *et al.* (1999) shows how behavioural patterns exhibited by buyers and sellers differ with different degrees of relationship quality. The study is of much use as far as dimensions of buyer-seller relationship quality and their interactions are concerned. But it has certain limitations like small sample size and lack of its representativeness as all the respondents belong to the same category.

Reddy and Czepiel (1999) in their paper entitled "Measuring and Modeling the Effects of Long Term Buyer-Seller Relationships in Corporate Financial Services Markets" give insight into the determinants of Long term relationships and the impact of those relationships on future performance. Data regarding the focal and few other banks has been collected through questionnaire and interviews administered by professional interviewers. A limitation of their study that is expected to be covered in the proposed research is that it focuses on only the important customers' of the bank.

JUSTIFICATION

Today banks are facing competition from other domestic and foreign banks, financial institutions and also other industries to attract personal dispensable income of the people. Moreover, the induction of technology, rising consumerism and a shift in consumer psychology has led banks to accept marketing of their services as an imperative. The proposed study is expected to provide direction in this regard by assessing the impact of the Relationship Marketing strategies being adopted by banks at present and suggesting new efforts to make them more effective. This would help the banks to alter their service package according to the changing customer's expectations and thus establish long term relationships with them. Moreover, most of the studies reviewed are conducted in affluent economies like U.S.A. and they concentrate on the identification of determinants of Relationship Marketing in insurance and financial services in general, impact of different types of buyer-seller interactions or encounters on relationship quality, etc. The proposed study is expected to encompass much more by evaluating the overall services rendered by Indian banks vis-a-vis banker-customers relationships, while at the same time concentrating on the various variables responsible for strengthening this relationship and finally, suggesting a relevant strategy that will be of more use to Indian banks.

OBJECTIVES

The similar research work should aim at attaining the following objectives:

Crosby and Stephens (1987) find that Relationship Marketing adds value to the service by providing certain peripherals. Also, Surprenant and Solomon (1987) and Susheela Devi (1995) have suggested systematic schemes of personalization and better customer service respectively. All this indicates the necessity of suggesting a strategy based on relevant peripherals strengthening Relationship Marketing efforts. Hence,

01. To work out a Relationship Marketing strategy for the development and maintenance of various needed peripherals relevant to Indian consumer banking services.

According to Diogo Teixeira and Joseph Ziskin (1993) banks are increasingly providing customer relationship training to their employees. As training entails extra cost and time, it is necessary to ensure if it is important or not. Hence,

02. To find the importance of training the employees for Relationship Marketing.

Texeira and Ziskin (1993) state that apart from training the bank employees they need to be empowered at the point of customer contact to make decisions. However, it does not mention whether bank staff other than primary contact persons are also instrumental in building relationships with customers. Hence, the next objective is:

03. To find at what levels in the organizational hierarchy of a bank, Relationship Marketing is practised.

According to Surprenant and Solomon (1987) customized personalization has positive effect on customer satisfaction and his impression about the service and service provider. However, it is also important to know whether the customers want services especially tailored for them or the same service as everybody else is being offered. Hence,

04. To find out whether customers prefer customized or standardized services.

Mookerjee and Shainesh (2000) point out that even the customers who are satisfied with the service switch to competing services. Thus, the fifth objective is:

05. To find out if customers with whom sound relations have been developed also defect and under what circumstances.

Kotler (1998) has given a 5 step 'Relationship-Marketing Programme' for companies. However, such a programme is suggested taking into consideration the American milieu. So, its applicability in Indian consumer banking needs to be tested in the light of global banking operations in India.

06. To find out whether the 'Relationship-Marketing Programme' given by Kotler is considered viable for Indian consumer banks.

According to Kolter (1999) companies must judge as to which segments and specific customers will respond profitably to relationship marketing. Also, Morgan and Hunt (1999) hold that relationship marketing should be adopted only when it offers, or contributes to, a firm's competitive advantage that proves sustainable. Hence,

07. To identify the customer segments where relationship marketing will be most effective.

HYPOTHESES

The related work should be based on the following hypotheses:

Banks are increasingly providing training to their employees, so as to deliver error free statements and transaction handling. Apart from this, relationship marketing training is also being imparted. This results in overall customer satisfaction and retention (Teixeira and Ziskin 1993). Hence, the first hypothesis is:

H1. Relationship Marketing training positively affects customer satisfaction in the form of error free service and customer orientation.

Teixeira and Ziskin (1993) state that employees are being empowered to make decisions at the point of customer contact so as to improve customer interface. However, Crosby and Stephens (1987) find that the primary contact person is a 'peripheral service provider'. His performance affects satisfaction but only when the core service is satisfying. This statement is countered by Surprenant and Solomon (1987) who state that though the service provider is the last link in the chain of production, he is the one who conveys the personality of the service being offered. The strategy used by him affects the overall satisfaction with the service. Thus, though the entire organization is involved in building sound customer relations. But the importance of the primary contact person cannot be negated. The strategy used by him can make or mar the efforts of the entire organization. Thus, the second hypothesis is:

H2. Relationship Marketing has permeated the entire organization but it's hub lies in the primary contact person.

Mookerjee and Shainesh (2000) find that satisfaction is a necessary but not the sufficient condition for loyalty. When taken together with relationship strength determinants like trust and commitment, it will lead to loyalty. Sometimes satisfied customers defect due to lack of sound relations with bank though it has been able to provide satisfactory services. Thus, sound relations help to retain customers. This leads to the next hypothesis:

H3. Customers with whom sound relations have been developed do not switch to competitors.

Surprenant and Solomon (1987) conducted a study by varying the type and degree of personalization in simulated banking transactions and inferred that customized personalization had uniformly positive effects on customer's evaluation of the service provider and his bank. Also, option personalization increased customers trust in the bank and satisfaction with his offerings. Hence,

H4. Option and customized personalization strategies increase customer satisfaction and trust.

Reddy and Czepiel (1999) studied the importance of long term relationship as a source of future sale and found out that longer relations have a positive effect on future usage of a product or service. The study suggests that in the presence of a strong relationship with customers, their propensity to leave the relationship is very low. This leads to the fifth hypothesis :

H5. Long term banker-customer relationship has a positive impact on future business.

Jap *et al.* (1999) studied the behavioural patterns exhibited by buyers and sellers and identified certain dimensions of relationship quality viz., trust, term orientation, conflict and disengagement level. Hence,

H6. High quality banker customer relationship exhibits high level of trust, longer term orientation and low conflict and disengagement levels.

RESEARCH DESIGN AND METHODOLOGY

The study ought to be descriptive, evaluative and diagnostic in nature. It should aim at finding out the impact of relationship marketing on satisfaction and loyalty of bank customers and proposing an apt strategy for relationship marketing. It should be descriptive because the domain of customer satisfaction and loyalty in consumer banking services in Indian settings needs to be explored from the present literature and on going banking practices.

Similarly, the extent, quality and effectiveness of relationship marketing have to be evaluated in terms of customer and executive opinions based on their experiences and judgements.

On the basis of the weak and strong points emerging from the study of the impact of marketing efforts of banks, a diagnostic strategy should be suggested for establishing effective relationship marketing (Nelson 1982).

Nature and Sources of Information

Primary information required for the study ought to be collected from bank customers of different market segments and bank staff at all levels through personal interviews and questionnaires. The secondary information need to be collected from RBI Bulletins, Statistical Tables, Basic Banking Statistics, Reports on Trend and Progress of Banking in India, annual reports of concerned banks, IBA Bulletins.

Generation of Scale Items

Seven point Likert scales (7<........>1) should be used to measure the responses of the respondents (Beri 1997). The scale items need to be generated with the help of literature reviewed and discussions with experts in the field. The scale items ought to cover the assessment of relationship marketing efforts by both bankers and their customers, evaluation of different services rendered, comparison with other banks, areas of inefficiencies, measurement of various dimensions and determinants of relationship strength, loyalty, satisfaction, etc. (Churchill 1983).

Purification of Scale Items

The scales should be factor analyzed with the help of SPSS package. After several iterations, final factors should be selected such that items with high loadings on more than one factor and those with loadings less than 0.5 should be ignored (Aaker and Day 1986 and Kaur 1999).

Data Collection Device

Data should be collected with the help of structured non-disguised questionnaires (Beri 1997). Two different sets of questionnaires should be designed for the collection of data from bank staff and their customers (Mishra 1998).

Selection of Respondents

Atleast 500 respondents (bank customers) should be selected on the basis of systematic random sampling. These areas for data collection ought to be purposely selected for being inhabited by urban banking customers availing majority of modern banking services offered. About 100 bankers should also be contacted for the data pertaining to their efforts for relationship marketing.

Pretesting

The questionnaire need to be pretested with 10% of the total sample size to identify improvements and modifications needed as per the research objectives.

Data Analysis and Statistical Tools

The scales give a series of quantitative data, corresponding to the responses of the respondents, which should be condensed with the help of arithmetic mean so as to facilitate analysis of data. Correlation and regression should be used to find out the nature of relation between relationship marketing efforts of bank and levels of customer satisfaction and loyalty (Boyd *et al.* 1988).

Reliability and Validity

The reliability of the multiple item scales used to measure satisfaction, loyalty, effectiveness of relationship marketing efforts should be estimated using internal consistency procedure (Nelson 1982). The sample should be divided into different categories on the basis of age, income, qualification, occupation, etc. and x^2 test should be used to test whether satisfaction level is equally distributed in various groups. Further the level of dimension-wise impact of relationship marketing on satisfaction and loyalty has to be tested with F-test.

Content validity need to be taken care of judgement from reference of all possible items (Nelson 1982) that come up during the process of literature survey, discussions with bankers and other knowledgeable people vis-a-vis pilot study.

LIMITATIONS

The study should be considered in the light of the following limitations:

1. While making the study area and market specific, a major section of bank customers residing in rural India may remains outside the sample.
2. The study concentrates on the impact of marketing relationships in consumer banking thus excluding corporate banking services.
3. The conclusions would be based on the responses obtained from the respondents through survey. Though utmost care should be taken to entice correct information, an element of subjectivity cannot be ruled out.
4. The study pertaining to consumer banking services in selected cities of the country cannot be generalized for whole of consumer banking industry.
5. The study may not only be area and market specific, but also time specific i.e. its findings may not be truly relevant to the on going process of 'cash less consumer banking operations' after some time even in the given area and market without making needed changes in its application.

PLAN OF PROPOSED WORK

The similar research work should be divided into the following chapters:

Introduction

The first chapter should explain the concept of 'Relationship Marketing'. It should also make clear the need and importance of relationship marketing for banks.

Review of Literature

Relevant existing literature need to be reviewed to find out the research gap to be bridged by the proposed study. This chapter should also facilitate the formulation of research objectives and hypotheses.

Research Design and Methodology

This chapter ought to mention the various steps taken to accomplish research objectives viz., information gathering, scale generation and purification, limitations of the study, etc.

Efforts of Relationship Marketing

It should bring to light various relationship marketing efforts being undertaken by banks and also those additional efforts which are suggested by the customers.

Customer Satisfaction

Customer satisfaction need to be measured separately for areas selected, different target markets, and various services provided and then compared to the expected satisfaction levels.

Customer Loyalty

The cause and effect relationships of customer loyalty to different banks should be identified in the sixth chapter so that appropriate relationship marketing strategy can be worked out.

Effectiveness of Relationship Marketing

The seventh chapter should assess the effectiveness of relationship marketing by comparing the marketing efforts of the banks with the satisfaction and loyalty, levels as identified in the previous chapters.

Strategy for Relationships Marketing

The last chapter should present an appropriate strategy for relationship marketing which will be formulated on the basis of the gaps identified in the marketing efforts of the banks, gaps in actual and expected levels of customer satisfaction and loyalty and also the suggestions made by the customers and bankers for the improvement of existing marketing efforts.

REFERENCES

1. Aaker and Day (1986), *Marketing Research,* John Wiley and Sons, Hongkong, pp. 444-448.
2. Beri, G.C. (1996), *Marketing Research,* Tata McGraw-Hill, New Delhi, pp. 101-148.
3. Boyd, Westfall and Stasch (1988), *Marketing Research,* Virendra Kumar Arya, Delhi, pp. 562-569.
4. Churchill, Gilbert A. (1983), *Marketing Research Methodological Foundations,* The Dryden Press, New Delhi, pp. 255-258.
5. Crosby, Lawrence A. and Nancy Stephens (1987), "Effects of Relationship Marketing on Satisfaction, Retention and prices in the Life Insurance Industry", in *Journal of Marketing Research,* Vol. 24, (November), pp. 404-411.
6. Devi, A. Susheela (1995) "Bank's Strategies to Entice More Customers", in N.Vinayakam (ed.), *Indian Banking by 2000A.D.,* pp. 196-202.
7. Jap, S. D *et. al.* (1999)., "Relationship Quality and Buyer-Seller Interactions in Channels of Distributions", *Journal of Business Research',* Vol. 46, No. 3, pp. 303-313.
8. Kaur, Gurjeet (1999), Marketing Orientation for Regional Rural Banks in Northern India- A Case Study of J&K and Punjab States (An unpublished Ph.D. Thesis in Jammu University), p. 53.

9. Kotler, Philip (1999), *Marketing Management,* Prentice-Hall of India, New Delhi, pp. 13-641.

10. Kotler, Philip (1998), *Marketing Management: Analysis, Planning, Implementation and Control,* Prentice-Hall of India, New Delhi, pp. 711-713.

11. Mishra, M.N. (1998), *Modern Marketing Research*, Himalaya Publishing House, pp. 126-132.

12. Mishra, Randhir (2000), "Satisfaction in Service Relationships: *A* Case for Professional Services", in M.Raghavachari and K.V. Ramani (eds.), *Delivering Service Quality,* Macmillan, New Delhi, pp. 610-615.

13. Mookerjee, Amit and G. Shainesh (2000), "Developing Measures for Service Quality and Relationship Strength Determinants of Customer Loyalty", in M.Raghavachari and K.V. Ramani (eds.) *Delivering Service Quality,* Macmillan, New Delhi, pp. 29-35.

14. Morgan, Robert M. and Shelby Hunt (1999), "Relationship Based Competitive Advantage: The Role of Relationship Marketing Strategy", *Journal of Business Research,* Vol. 46, No. 3, pp. 281-290.

15. Nelson, James E.(1992), *The Practice of Marketing Research*, Kent Publishing Company, California, pp. 257-265.

16. Panigrahy, Dibakar (2000), "Relationship Marketing: An Opportunity for Bankers in the Next Millenium", in M. Raghavachari and K.V. Ramani (eds.), *Delivering Service Quality,* Macmillan, New Delhi, pp. 85-91.

17. Ramaswamy, V.S. and Namakumari (1995), *Marketing Management, Planning, Implementation and Control—The Indian Context*, p. 184.

18. Reddy, Srinivas K. and John A. Czepiel (1999), "Measuring and Modeling the Effects of Long Term Buyer- Seller Relationship in Corporate Financial Service Markets", *Journal of Business Research,* Vol. 46, No. 3, pp. 235-244.

19. Suprenant, Carol F. and Michael R. Solomon (1987), "Predictability and Personalisation in the Service Encounter", *Journal of Marketing*', (April), pp. 86-90.
20. Teixeira, Diogo and Joseph Ziskin (1993), "Achieving Quality with Customer in Mind", *The Banker's Magazine*, (January/February), pp. 29-35.

12

COMPETITIVE MARKETING STRATEGY FOR CUSTOMER SATISFACTION IN INDIAN CONSUMER BANKING

—R.D. SHARMA & JYOTI SHARMA

Globalisation, liberalisation and deregulation have resulted in sea change in the form of time and cost effective consumer banking services (Javalgi 1992). This ongoing process of change has made bank customers more and more knowledgeable and aware of their surrounding environment. The change in the customer expectations is due to the use of latest technology (e.g. internet, online marketing) by them so as to ferret different available alternatives from around the world and eventually arming themselves with an unprecedented amount of marketing knowledge (Parasuraman 2000). There has been a tremendous growth of domestic as well as multinational banks in India, the rise of which has led to a competitive environment. This competitive environment in consumer banking mounts the pressure on bankers to provide better and innovative service, thus implying that the bankers have not only to market the core services but also improve the quality of services provided so as to ensure customer satisfaction (Parasuraman *et al.* 1998) and retention.

Competition on the basis of superior customer service offers a solid foundation for erecting and enduring competitive edge (Parasuraman 2000). Moreover, the progress of service providers depends on the customer satisfaction and service quality in all developing and developed countries (Sharma and Chahal 1999).

Today's globalised market has given a new meaning to the concept of quality. Though focus today is on satisfying the customers, which has led to a new view of quality related to product/service development and to the delivery process. The bankers want to understand what is behind customer satisfaction so that they can meet or exceed customer expectations, which win lead to higher profitability and customer loyalty. (Teixeiro and Ziskin 1993).

Marketing in banks came in the last 1950's in the form of advertising and promotional concept. In India, Banking within the framework of social marketing concept, has lead to create customer satisfaction and long run public and customer welfare schemes to satisfy the nations goals and responsibilities (Balasubramanian 1995). Resultantly customer satisfaction has also become a top priority in banking services. Time has come for adoption of a successful marketing strategy based on consumer expectation. Bankers require a strategy, which makes possible a fair blending of customers and bank interest. For instance Bankers need to offer right services to right customers, at the right time and at right price.

A shift in the customer expectation has made it necessary that bankers assign overriding priority to the formulation of innovative marketing strategies for bank services. Excelling in the market place on a sustained basis is impossible without excelling in service quality and customer satisfaction. Delivering quality service is considered an essential strategy for success and survival in today's competitive environment. (Zeithaml, Berry. Parasuraman 1996) because a satisfied customer becomes an unpaid salesman for the bank and customer satisfaction should be the aim of marketing strategy.

REVIEW OF LITERATURE

Claes Fornell (1992) in his paper "A National Customer Satisfaction Barometer: The Swedish Experience" has formulated customer satisfaction barometer which is an index based on the data collected from more than 100 companies in 30 different industries over a period of three years. Information was gathered through telephonic interviews from randomly selected Swedish firms. The paper however, does not indicate the factors influencing the customer satisfaction. This gap will be filled in by identifying the factors affecting customers satisfaction and suggesting measures for improving it.

Rajshekhar G. Javalgi (1992) in his paper "Marketing Financial Services to Affluent Consumers" tries to understand the affluent customer wants through the marketing concept. He uses segmentation approach to reveal the behaviour of affluent and non-affluent segment members towards the financial institutions. The respondents were randomly selected from a telephone directory. The study has been conducted in affluent economies. The proposed study will be conducted in India and will identify the needs and wants to bank customers of different demographic profiles.

Shainesh and Mathur (2000) in their paper "Service Quality Measurement: The Case of Railway Freight Services" have identified the attributes which the customer used for evaluating the quality of freight services provided by the Railways. Data was collected from 51 customer organizations of 13 different industries through interviews with managers of such firms, which had used these services atleast once in previous six months. The paper does not have a transparent methodology and is also not explicit about how the dimensions for the RAILQUAL were selected.

Parasuraman's (2000) paper entitled "Superior Customer Service and Marketing Excellence: Two sides of the Same Success Coin": advances argument for broadening the scope of marketing to include customer satisfaction and demonstrates a judicious blending of conventional marketing and service quality for market success. The research continued for 15 years involving 15 industries in 40 different countries. The SERVQUAL will be used in the proposed study. Since the research was conducted over 15 years during which there might have been certain changes in the consumer expectations, perceptions and behavior that have not yet been studied. The proposed study tends to explore such changes in the consumers in the light of ongoing process of globalisation.

Parasuraman, Zeithaml and Berry (1985) in their paper "A Conceptual Model of Service Quality and Its Implication for Future Research" conducted an exploratory research to investigate the concept of service quality. Focus group interviews with consumers and in depth interviews with executives of 4 nationally recognised US services firms were conducted to develop conceptual model of service quality. Insights obtained from such interviews formed the basis of a model that summarises the nature and determinants of services quality as perceived by consumers. The ten determinants identified viz. reliability, responsiveness, courtesy and communication etc. will be taken up in the proposed research.

JUSTIFICATION

The continuous process of globalization, deregulation, liberalization (Javalgi 1992) has made the bank customer more and more knowledgeable and aware of his surrounding environment. With the use of the latest technology, the customer expectations have undergone a change as they keep themselves armed with the unprecedented amount of market knowledge (Parasuraman 2000). Such a market pressure on the business forces the marketer to keep their customers satisfied. The concept of satisfaction has led to the growing focus on service quality on competitive basis.

This process of ongoing change in the expectation of customers and the constant innovation in banking services could necessitate the similar work. Moreover, majority of research work have been conducted in affluent economies and not much work has been done in developing economies particularly in Indian consumer banking. The similar work should prove to be an asset to bankers, policy makers as well as bank customers. With the introduction of customer satisfaction in banking services, customer needs would be given top priority, which would ultimately enable the banks to earn long-term profits and achieve socio-economic objectives. The greater customer satisfaction, greater would be customer loyalty and greater repeat business in this era of competition.

OBJECTIVES

The similar research work should aim at achieving the following objectives formulated from the research gaps identified from the above literature reviewed:

(i) With the ongoing process of globalisation the bank customer expectations have undergone a tremendous change due to greater emphasis on service quality and information technology in the backdrop of ongoing banking reforms and global quality service (Javalgi 1992, Parasuraman 2000). Therefore, it has become essential for the bankers to continuously maintain high level of customer satisfaction with such a fast increasing track of service quality. This leads to the first objective of the research work i.e.:

To determine the nature and extent of customer satisfaction in Indian Customer Banking.

(ii) Parasuraman (1985), a pioneer in service quality, has undertaken a lot of research work for identification of major determinants of service quality in general where banking services were not given due representation. This research gap leads to the second objective:

To ascertain whether all the determinants of SERVQUAL provided by Parasuraman are equally important and applicable in today's banking services.

(iii) Today is the era of customer delight: Companies in order to achieve a competitive marketing edge are not content with customer satisfaction only but aim for customer delight (Kotler 1999) which has not been empirically studied. Hence, the next objective:

To determine the factors affecting customer satisfaction as well as customer delight.

(iv) Zeithaml, Berry and Parasuraman (1996) conducted research to ascertain the impact of service quality on behavioral pattern of customers but its relationship with customer satisfaction and loyalty has got to be examined, thereby leading to fourth objective:

To study the impact of service quality on customer loyalty and satisfaction.

(v) Samson E. Edo (1999) undertook a research in Nigeria to identify the important factors that influence customer choice of bank in urban areas but does not identify factors leading to customer satisfaction. Thus, this research gap leads to next objective:

To determine the impact of the factors identified by Edo on customer satisfaction in Indian consumer banking.

(vi) The present level of customer satisfaction may not remain even customer's expectation by tomorrow due to the fast changes in the expectation regarding quality, services and technology in banking services. The ongoing process of change in measuring and maintaining customer satisfaction requires formulation of regularly updated competitive marketing action plan to keep pace with these market changes in service business. Thus the next objective:

> To work out a suitable competitive marketing strategy for creating and enhancing customer satisfaction with the pace of increase in service quality in Indian consumer banking.

HYPOTHESES

The review of existing literature has resulted in the formulation of following hypotheses for the present study:

(i) Sharma & Chahal (1999) in their study entitled, "A study of Patient Satisfaction in Outdoor Service of Private Health Care Facilities" have quantified patient (customer) satisfaction on the basis of primary data gathered through five point Likert scale from 220 randomly selected patients of outdoor services in the private health care facilities as 3.47. Similarly Tandon (1996) in her study entitled, "Organizational Behaviour of Banking Sector in India" has also estimated customer satisfaction on the basis of first hand information gathered from customers of four banks in Jammu city as 3.32. All this facilitates the setting up of first hypothesis as—

> A moderate level of customer satisfaction prevails in banking services.

(ii) Parasuraman (2000) in his study entitled, "Superior Customer Services and Marketing Excellence: Two

Sides of the Same Success Coin", undertook extensive research and conducted empirical studies of several sectors to develop and refine SERVQUAL, a multi item instrument to quantify the service expectation gap along five dimensions viz. reliability, responsiveness, assurance, empathy and tangibility. This leads to setting up of next hypothesis:

> All the determinants of SERVQUAL given by Parasuraman play an important role in achieving customer satisfaction in banking services.

(iii) Javalgi (1992) in his study conducted in Nigeria entitled "Marketing Financial Services to Affluent Consumers" uses a segmentation approach in understanding consumer satisfaction/dissatisfaction among affluent and non-affluent customers of these services and finds that both the segments have different expectations from the services received. Thus the next hypothesis:

> The degree of customer satisfaction in consumer banking varies in accordance with the socio-economic background of the customers.

(iv) Zeithaml, Berry and Parasuraman (1996) in their paper entitled "The Behavioral Consequences of Services Quality" have examined the relationship of customer behavioural intentions such as loyalty, switch, pay more, etc. and service quality. The findings of the study revealed that there exists a positive link between service quality and behavior intentions. This facilitates the fourth hypothesis:

> Service quality has a positive impact on customer satisfaction and loyalty.

(v) Samson E. Edo (1999) in his paper entitled "Urban Customers Choice of Bank in Less Developed

Countries" has through field research conducted in Nigeria, identified fourteen factors such as liquidity, location, security, speed of services, etc. that determine patronage by customers. This results in setting up of next hypotheses:

> In today's competitive environment the factors identified by Edo in Nigerian banking services are equally important in Indian setting.

RESEARCH DESIGN AND METHODOLOGY

The related research work should be both diagnostic and evaluative in nature. The study should aim at estimating the nature and extent of customer satisfaction through both executives as well as customer evaluative judgment, which has to be duly counter-checked with the existing research evidences and also empirically. Similar inbuilt diagnostic process of research should result in formulation of a strategic action plan based on the directions drawn from the investigation conducted.

In the light of the aforesaid objectives and hypothesis formulated, the various relevant aspects of the research methodology are as under:

(i) Nature and Source of Information

For measuring the nature and extent of customer satisfaction in Indian consumer banking vis-a-vis formulating strategic action plan for improving and maintaining competitive marketing efforts, both primary and secondary information (Beri 1993 and Churchill 1983) need to be gathered from all relevant sources. It is only the ultimate users of consumer banking services who are more experienced and knowledgeable about the effectiveness of marketing efforts in rendering satisfaction to them. (Sharma 1996) and therefore, they need to be contacted for relevant information. Similarly for authenticity and internal status of these efforts the bankers operating in the areas under reference should also be requested to supply the relevant information. Further, the secondary information regarding various banking products like deposits, loans and customer services like bank draft, lockers facilities, etc. should be taken from related literature as well as bank publications viz. RBI bulletin, IBA bulletin, reports on trends and progress of banking in India etc. available at RBI and other bank libraries and bank training centers.

(ii) Selection of Respondents

The primary information should be collected from a sample of at least 500 households. The locations for the collection of relevant data ought to be purposely taken, which should represent the experienced bank customers belonging to various demographic groups who avail all types of consumer banking services available within the Indian banking system. The respondents should be selected through systematic random sampling (Beri 1996) i.e. the first house at random and subsequently every tenth house from each of the locations. Similarly for counter-checking and to have perceptual understanding of bank management, a sample of about 200 bank managers would serve the purpose.

(iii) Construction of Data Collection Forms

Since the study confines to evaluation of existing consumer banking services, the first hand information should be gathered from the experienced and knowledgeable bank customers (Churchill 1983) through such a multi-item seven point pre-tested and well structured questionnaire which provides inbuilt consistency, reliability and validity of data (Mishra 1998). As per the procedures and guidelines followed in the updated SERVQUAL (Parasuraman 2000), RAILQUAL (Shainesh and Mathur 2000), MKTEFFECT (Sharma 1996), Edo's work (1999) etc., a draft questionnaire need to be prepared for collecting information about customer expectation and bank product/service performance so that the real evaluative net result/difference between expectation and performance (Parasuraman, Zeithaml, Berry 1985), leading to either satisfaction or delight or dissatisfaction could objectively be found out besides covering basic general information for group comparisons. Similarly, another questionnaire for internal counter check on the relevance of the study need to be developed for gathering information from the bankers operating in the locations selected for the study.

(iv) Generation of Scale Items

The whole domain of customer satisfaction in consumer banking services to be measured through customer judgment and bank executives opinion need to be covered through all its possible dimensions in the form of seven point scaled items (7<....> 1) regarding quality of service performance. Thus large number of statements on the given scale should be generated from the existing literature in consultation with the experts. The scale items should cover all the consumer banking services falling within the framework of extended marketing mix (Kotler 1999). Besides, the queries about the demographic profiles of the respondents and about such aspects like length of association with prime bank and other banks etc. should also be obtained from the existing literature.

(v) Scale Purification

Before drawing statistical inferences, the seven point Likert Scale being followed, need to be purified in the several iterations through data reduction technique of factor analysis based on Principal axis procedure and Varimax rotation. The technique with the help of SPSS needs to be repeatedly carried on till the relative importance of every item of the scale is significantly recognised with at least 0.5 factor loading.

(vi) Pretesting

Before collecting the needed data from aforesaid samples

of respondents, both the questionnaires should be subjected to a pilot study (Beri 1996) by gathering needed information from about 5% of the sample size in both the cases in the same manner as explained under the section selection of respondents.

(vii) Measurement of Customer Satisfaction

Customer satisfaction, being qualitative phenomenon experienced by the users of the services, should be measured on a seven point Likert scale ranging from best level of performance to the poorest level of performance in every type of banking services provided to the customer. This technique of measurement (Tull & Hawkins 1998) ought to be applied for all groups of respondents in all types of banking services taken in the study. The consolidated level of satisfaction in such a case need to be measured through arithmetic mean and nature of relationship between customer satisfaction and various independent variables like product package delivery systems, marketing communication, etc. should be established through multiple regression.

(viii) Reliability and Validity

The value of dimension-wise, variable-wise, and group-wise customer satisfaction ought to be tested convergently with overall satisfaction under each of these characteristics for finding its validity. The level of dimension-wise impact on overall customer satisfaction for each variable should be tested with 'F' test, the level of significance in contributing to the degree of overall customer satisfaction has to be determined with the help of 't' test. The strength of the factors, which will finally emerge important for the study, has to be determined in terms of level of variance and extent of loadings of different statements on the factors explained with the help of factor analysis. Moreover, split half procedure should also be applied to determine the internal consistency in the findings (Churchill 1983).

PLAN FOR THE PROPOSED WORK

The similar work should be divided into following chapters each covering a significant part of the study. It is explained as under:

(i) The introductory chapter of the study should be devoted to the historical growth and development of the concept of customer satisfaction with special reference to services in general and consumer banking services in particular. Besides, the global position, the present status of research in India should also be examined in the background of the ongoing banking reforms so that the relevance of the research to the society, planners and academicians is clearly justified.

(ii) In the second chapter, "Review of Literature" the existing literature gap ought to be traced from both pioneer as well as recent studies on customer satisfaction in general and in consumer banking services in particulars by reviewing the research work of Parasuraman, Zeithaml, Berry, Shainesh, Javalgi, Samson Edo, Sharma, etc.

(iii) The third chapter on "Research design and methodology" should consist of a detailed description of the methodology adopted for the study under various heading viz. objectives, hypothesis, etc. so as to explain in detail as to what the study aims to achieve, the statistical tools applied, how the results have been obtained, the reliability, validity of research, so that source of data collected and methodology adopted become transparent and explicit.

(iv) Customer satisfaction regarding various deposits options available to the customers' needs to be examined in chapter fourth. It should provide deposit-wise cum respondent group-wise nature and extent of customer satisfaction along with the appropriate marketing action plan for better functioning of the concerned banks regarding various deposit accounts.

(v) Extent of customer satisfaction in lending operations comprising all the major aspects of loan schemes like loan procedures, loan options, repayments of principal and interest, etc. should be estimated in fifth chapter. On the basis of the evaluative results a strategy for better loan services should also be given in this chapter.

(vi) Besides, deposit and loan schemes, various other banking services like locker facilities, collection of bills, ATM, home/tele banking, credit cards, bank draft, etc. ought to be studied in chapter sixth. Accordingly, a strategy for creating and maintaining high customer satisfaction should also be presented in this chapter.

(vii) An overall competitive marketing strategy for customer satisfaction in Indian consumer banking need to be consolidated in the last chapter on the basis of major findings about the strength and weaknesses in the ongoing marketing efforts as evaluated in terms of customer satisfaction methodology adopted in the preceding chapters.

LIMITATIONS AND PRECAUTIONS

The research for the formulation of competitive marketing strategy for customer satisfaction in Indian consumer banks has to be based on multifaceted information from different sources. Similarly, the findings duly supported with tests of validity, reliability and consistency should be quite transparent and objectives. But such a research exercise passes through several limitations for which if appropriate precautions are not taken the study remains unacceptable and invalid. Thus various limitations are discussed as under along with the steps to be taken during the entire study:

(i) Since the topic of research is connected with the private information regarding bank services, viz., deposits, loans and other supportive services, the respondents both the ultimate consumers and the bankers are likely to hide the information.

(ii) The study is of such a nature that it tends to reflect the efforts put in by the bankers to enhance customer's satisfaction. However, when contacted the bankers may project a better and exaggerated picture of the services provided which quite possibly would be the opposite to actual service provided. This would result in misleading the research.

The aforesaid problems should be dealt by drafting the questionnaire with protective and disguised questions duly supported with internal checks and it should also be counter-checked by customers and bankers.

(iii) The Indian consumer banks are operating in the entire country through more than 65000 branches and extending all the modern banking services. Thus in order to cover the entire major banking services ought to be purposely selected for the collection of primary information.

(iv) Customer satisfaction is a qualitative phenomenon for which direct and accurate measurement is difficult. It should be measured through self-developed seven point Likert scale multi item questionnaire covering the entire domain of the topic in question.

(v) The topic of research deals with the entire consumer banking industry in India for which a reasonably large sample comprising all segments of markets needs to be selected through a random sampling technique by ensuring the characteristics of the research population. A sample of about 500 customers and 200 bank managers ought to be selected in such a way that they represent the whole research population characteristics.

REFERENCES

Balasubramanian, C.S. (1995), "Bank Marketing and Public Relation." *IBI Bulletin,* September, pp. 13-15.

Beri, G.C. (1996), *Marketing Research,* Tata McGraw Hill, New Delhi, pp. 48-163.

Churchill Gilbert, A. (1983), *Marketing Research Methodological Foundations.* The Dryden Press, New Delhi, pp. 170-621.

Edo, Samson. E. (1999), "Urban Customers' Choice of Bank in Less Developed Countries." *The Journal of Business Perspective,* (Jan. - June), pp. 42- 47.

Fornell, Claes (1992), "A National Customer Satisfaction Barometer: The Swedish Experience." *The Journal of Marketing* (6 January), pp. 6-19.

Javalgi, Rajshekhar, G. (1992), "Marketing Financial Services to Affluent Consumers," *The Journal of Service Marketing,* Vol. 6, No. 2, pp. 33-44.

Kotler, Philip (1999), *Marketing Management,* Prentice-Hall of India Private Limited, New Delhi, p. 36.

Mishra, M.N. (1998), *Modern Marketing Research,* Himalaya Publishing House, pp. 120-134.

Parasuraman, A. (2000), "Superior Customer Service and Marketing Excellence: Two Sides of the Same Success Coin," *Vikalpa,* Vol. 25, No. 3, (July-Sept.), pp. 3-13.

Parasuraman. A, Zeithaml and Berry (1985), "A Conceptual Model of Service Quality and its Implication for Future Research", *Journal of Marketing*. Vol. 49, pp. 41-50.

Shainessh, G. and Mukul Mathur (2000), "Service Quality Measurement: The Case of Railway Freight Services", *Vikalpa,* Vol. 25, No. 3, (July-Sept.), pp. 15-22.

Sharma, R.D and Hardeep Chahal (1999), "A Study of Patient Satisfaction in Outdoor Services of Private Health Care Facilities", *Vikalpa,* Vol. 24, No. 4 (October-December), pp. 69-76.

Sharma, R.D. (1996), "MKTEFFECT: A Multi Item Scale for Measuring Marketing Effectiveness in American Consumer Banking Through Customer Judgement", *Vikalpa,* Vol. 21, No. l, (Jan.-March), pp. 57-68.

Tandon, Sandeep (2001), *Organisational Behaviour of Banking Sector in India,* Mohit Publications, New Delhi, pp. 150-160.

Teixeiro, Diogo and Joseph Ziskin (1993), 'Achieving Quality with Customers in Mind', *The Bankers Magazine* (Jan.-Feb.), pp. 29-31.

Tull, Donald, Hawkins Del (1998), *Marketing Research Measurement and Method,* Prentice-Hall of India Private Limited, New Delhi, pp. 298.

Zeithaml, Berry and Parasuraman (1996), "The Behavioral Consequences of Service Qualityt", *Journal of Marketing,* Vol. 60, pp. 31-46.

INDEX

❑❑❑